Frances Hopwood has taught English in Malawi, Central Africa, and English as a Foreign Language at Waltham Forest College, London. She currently teaches English as a Foreign Language at Ealing College of Higher Education, London, and supervises trainee teachers on RSA TEFL courses.

djamal @ awael68
Free serve. co. uk.

Also available

Companion French Grammar
Companion German Grammar
Companion Spanish Grammar

First published 1988 by Pan Books Ltd.
Cavaye Place, London SW10 9PG
1 2 3 4 5 6 7 8 9

ISBN 0 330 29778 3
Editor: Adrian Stenton
Photoset by Rowland Phototypesetting Ltd.,
Bury St Edmunds, Suffolk
Printed and bound in Great Britain by
Richard Clay Ltd., Bungay, Suffolk

Companion English Grammar

FRANCES HOPWOOD

Pan Books London, Sydney and Auckland

Contents

How to use this book

The *Companion English Grammar* is a simple reference book for students of English who want to be able to check their use of language quickly and easily – and you don't have to know about grammar to be able to use it.

Topics are presented on a double page to make them easy to follow. They have been chosen because the author has found that they are the ones that students usually have problems with.

This is a grammar book that you can carry around with you and actually use all the time. If you need help when you're:

- talking to people
- using the telephone
- writing a letter

then you need this book.

If you want to know:

- how to form the present perfect tense
- if you can you use this tense form to describe an action that has finished
- how to form a question with *do*
- when to use *more* and *most* and when to use *-er* and *-est*

this book will tell you, and give you plenty of examples to follow.

The layout of this book makes these things very easy to find. You can:

- use the **Contents**
- use the **Index**
- **skim** through the book, looking at the example boxes

So even if you don't know the name of what you're looking for, this book will help you to find it.

For example, if you are looking for a verb form with *have*, you can:

Look in the *Contents*. Here you'll find all of the structures and forms listed with page references:

Look in the *Index*. Here you'll find all of the structures, forms and words listed in alphabetical order with page references:

Skim through the book, looking at the examples. This is useful if you're not sure what you're looking for. You'll find:

She **has** two brothers.

The bus **has** just **left**.

When you turn to a section, you'll find helpful information about how to use the tense, phrase or word and lots of example sentences for you to follow or copy.

At the back of the book are some additional helpful sections:

- a list of irregular verbs so that you can quickly check the verb you want
- a glossary of grammatical terms to help you find your way around this and other grammars.

To Be

I **am** a student.

Use *to be* as an ordinary verb:

to give information about people or things:

She's a computer operator.
It was his birthday last week, wasn't it?
They're in their room.

to describe people and situations:

He isn't very well.
Was he late for school this morning? Yes, he was.
The roads were very busy. It took us ages to get back.

Use *it* + *be* to talk about the time and the date, and about the weather and distances:

What time is it? It's half past ten.
What's the date today? It's January 3.
It was cold yesterday but it's warmer today.
It's nearly 200 kilometres to London from here.

Use *there* + *be* to say that something exists:

There's some more milk in the fridge if you need it.
There were six people waiting when I got to the shop.
There wasn't much traffic this morning.

Use *be* with another verb to make the present continuous and past continuous tenses:

I can't come now; I'm cooking the dinner.
He was talking to his friend Steve when I last saw him.

Use *be* with another verb to make the passive:

Their car was stolen from outside our house.
The elephants are fed at 3.30 every afternoon.

Form

be was/were been being

Positive	Short forms	Negative	Short forms
I am	I'm	I am not	I'm not
You are	You're	You are not	You aren't
He/she/it is	He's/she's/it's	He/she/it is not	He/she/it isn't
We are	We're	We are not	We aren't
You are	You're	You are not	You aren't
They are	They're	They are not	They aren't

Questions	Negative questions
Am I?	Aren't I?
Are you?	Aren't you?

Answers	Negative answers
Yes, I am	No, I'm not

Past tense

Positive	Negative	Short forms
I was	I was not	I wasn't
You were	You were not	You weren't
He/she/it was	He/she/it was not	He/she/it wasn't
We were	We were not	We weren't
You were	You were not	You weren't
They were	They were not	They weren't

Questions	Negative questions
Were you?	Weren't you?

Answers	Negative answers
Yes, I was	No, I wasn't

Usage note

***be* is not usually used in continuous tenses, even when you might expect it to be used:**

I am happy just to lie in the sun.

To Do

Will you please **do** your homework!

Use *to do* as an ordinary verb:

to talk about an action:
She wants to know what to do.
What are you doing this evening?
What are you going to do in Wales?

to talk about work:
I'll do the cooking if you do the washing-up.
We've got to do our homework tonight.
He's doing languages at school.
What does she do? She's a doctor.

Use *do* with another verb to make questions:
Do you need anything from the shops?
Does she like jazz?
Did you know that the Odeon has closed?

Use *do* with another verb to make negatives:
I don't sing in the choir any more.
He doesn't usually tell anyone where he is.
We didn't notice any interesting places to stop.
They did not answer the questions truthfully.

Use *do* to order someone not to do something:
Don't move or I'll shoot.
Don't tell anyone. It's a secret.
Don't be silly!

Form

do did done doing

Positive	**Negative**	**Short forms**
I do	I do not	I don't
You do	You do not	You don't
He/she/it does	He/she/it does not	He/she/it doesn't
We do	We do not	We don't
You do	You do not	You don't
They do	They do not	They don't

Questions	**Negative questions**
Do you?	Don't you?

Answers	**Negative answers**
Yes, I do	No, I don't

Past tense

Positive	**Negative**	**Short forms**
I did	I did not	I didn't
You did	You did not	You didn't
He/she/it did	He/she/it did not	He/she/it didn't
We did	We did not	We didn't
You did	You did not	You didn't
They did	They did not	They didn't

Questions	**Negative questions**
Did you?	Didn't you?

Answers	**Negative answers**
Yes, I did	No, I didn't

To Have

She **has** two brothers.

Use *to have* as an ordinary verb:

to show possession, or a relationship, or a state:

He has two brothers.
They have lovely fresh bread in that shop.
Does she still have that old red car? Yes, she does.
They didn't have enough money to stay for two weeks.
I haven't had much work to do for several days.
Anna had a cold, so she didn't come with us.

to talk about actions:

Did you have a good holiday? Yes, it was wonderful.
We had some trouble with our car.
I had a very busy day yesterday.
I hope you have a good weekend in Scotland.
We're having a party on Saturday.
Have you had your dinner yet?
He's having a bath. He'll be down in a minute.
When do you have your guitar lesson?
John's just having a talk with Bill.

Usage note

You can also use *have got* to show possession, or a relationship, or a state:

Have you got a pen I can use? Sorry, I haven't.
I've got a coat you can borrow if you're cold.
He's so pleased. He's just got his exam results!
They've both got the flu so they won't be coming.
You haven't got his phone number, have you?

Use *have* with another verb to make the present perfect and past perfect tenses:

I've forgotten to bring my raincoat.
He's been here for two weeks.
We'd known him for three years when he died.
They'd phoned several times but no one had replied.

Use *have* with an object and past participle (*to have something done*) to show that you cause someone else to do something for you:

I have my hair cut every month.
(= My hairdresser cuts my hair for me every month.)
The house looks lovely. We had it painted recently.
(= A decorator came and painted the house for us.)
He can't come next week; he's having his car serviced.
(= The garage will service his car for him.)

Use *have to* or *have got to* to show obligation. It means the same as *must*:

I have to leave in a minute.
I've got to leave in a minute.
Do you have to finish all that work?
Have you got to finish all that work?
Where are Jo and Brian? They had to go early.
Why did they have to go? Jo had to get home by 6.

Use *had better* to give advice:

It's getting late. You'd better hurry.
I'd better phone my dad and wish him a happy birthday.
Hadn't you better ask first before you take his book?
We'd better not be late because he'll only get upset.

Form

have had had having

Positive	Short forms	Negative	Short forms
I have	I've	I have not	I haven't
You have	You've	You have not	You haven't
He/she/it has	He's/she's/it's	He/she/it has not	He/she/it hasn't
We have	We've	We have not	We haven't
You have	You've	You have not	You haven't
They have	They've	They have not	They haven't

Questions
Have you?

Negative questions
Haven't you?

Answers
Yes, I have

Negative answers
No, I haven't

Past tense

Positive	Short forms	Negative	Short forms
I had	I'd	I had not	I hadn't
You had	You'd	You had not	You hadn't
He/she/it had	He'd/she'd/it'd	He/she/it had not	He/she/it hadn't
We had	We'd	We had not	We hadn't
You had	You'd	You had not	You hadn't
They had	They'd	They had not	They hadn't

Questions
Had you?

Negative questions
Hadn't you?

Answers
Yes, I had

Negative answers
No, I hadn't

Usage note

***have you?* and *haven't you?*, *had you?* and *hadn't you?* are rather formal. Instead you can use *do you have?* and *don't you have?*, and *did you have?* and *didn't you have?*:**

Do you have any low-fat milk, please?
Did you have any luck at the races?

Tense and Time

In English there is not always a direct relationship between verb tense and time. For example, the present simple tense can be used to refer to both present and future time. In the list below, we tell you which tenses can be used to refer to past, present and future time. The forms and use of these tenses are shown in the next few pages.

Present time

Present simple: It always rains in England.
Present continuous: I'm listening to this play on the radio.

Past time

Past simple: She posted the letter to you two days ago.
Present perfect: The bus has just left.
Past perfect: After we had finished our meal, we paid the bill and left.
Past continuous: He was working in the garden at the weekend.
Present perfect continuous: John has been learning to play the piano for two years now.
Past perfect continuous: They had been walking all day when they reached the pub.

Future time

will: It will take two hours to get to Manchester.
be going to: He's going to leave his job at the end of the month.
Present simple: The film starts at 9 o'clock tomorrow evening.
Present continuous: I'm phoning my mother in Australia later.
Future perfect: The plane will have landed by now.
Future continuous: I'll be meeting them on Sunday.

Spelling note

Many English verbs have irregular forms. You will find a list of irregular verb forms on page 131.

Present Simple Tense

It always **rains** in England.

You use the present simple tense to talk about:

something which is true for a long time or always:

You drive on the left in Britain.
Cats love cream.
It rains a lot here in the spring.
We live in Manchester.
Do you take sugar? Yes, I do, please.

something which happens again and again, regularly:

I do my shopping every Saturday morning.
He often plays football at the weekend.
They usually visit their daughter once a month.
She catches the 8.35 bus to work every morning.

what you think or believe:

We believe the Council should spend more money on roads.
Do you know how to change the tyre? No, I don't.
He doesn't like his job; he wants to work abroad.
Does she want to come with us? Yes, she does.

how you feel and what you touch, hear, see and smell:

I feel ill; I want to sit down.
She loves horror films even though they frighten her.
That curry smells delicious; is it ready yet?
It looks like rain.
I see 'Jaws' is on at the Odeon next week.
That sounds good. Is it a new record?

You can also use the simple present to talk about the future:

The bus leaves at 6 o'clock and arrives in London at 9.
Anna starts work tomorrow.

Form

Positive
I like coffee
You like coffee
He/she/it likes coffee
We like coffee
You like coffee
They like coffee

Negative
I don't like coffee
You don't like coffee
He/she/it doesn't like coffee
We don't like coffee
You don't like coffee
They don't like coffee

Questions
Do you like coffee?
Does he/she/it like coffee?

Negative questions
Don't you like coffee?
Doesn't he/she/it like coffee?

Answers
Yes, I do
Yes, he/she/it does

Negative answers
No, I don't
No, he/she/it doesn't

Spelling notes

Verbs which end in *-ss*, *-sh*, *-ch*, or *-o*, use *-es* for the he/she/it form:

He washes his hair every day. (wash)
She watches a lot of television. (watch)
This car goes very well. (go)
The cat always hisses at dogs. (hiss)

Verbs which end in a consonant + *-y*, use *-ies* for the he/she/it form:

He worries a lot about his work. (worry)
The baby tries to stand up but falls over a lot. (try)

Usage notes

When things happen regularly, we often use these adverbs with the present simple tense:

always, usually, often, sometimes, occasionally, ever.

Some verbs, especially those which state feelings, beliefs and opinions, are used in the present simple tense, even when you might expect to use the present continuous:

I like lying in the sun.

Past Simple Tense

She **posted** the letter to you two days ago.

You use the past simple tense to talk about:

something which happened, or was true in the past, but which is now finished:

Thank you for a marvellous party; we enjoyed it very much.
The bus didn't come but I ran all the way and managed to get there just in time.
I felt tired so I decided to leave early.
Where did you first meet your wife?
He worked at Lucas Motors for four years.
I learned to drive when I was 18.
She lived abroad for many years.
I liked going to the horse races before I got married.

and to report what someone said:

He told me to come and see you.
They told me that I looked different.
She said she wanted to come with us.
I asked them where they lived.
Did you explain why we couldn't help?

Usage note

When you use a word or phrase which tells you when something happened or was true, e.g. *at 3 o'clock*, *yesterday*, *on 3rd June*, *on Thursday*, *two weeks ago*, *last month*, *in 1984*, *When . . .?*, you must use the simple past:

What did you do last weekend? Oh, we stayed at home.
I saw the film on TV last night: I thought it was very good.
She posted the letter to you two days ago.

Form

Positive	**Negative**
I worked hard	I didn't work hard
You worked hard	You didn't work hard
He/she/it worked hard	He/she/it didn't work hard
We worked hard	We didn't work hard
You worked hard	You didn't work hard
They worked hard	They didn't work hard
Questions	**Negative questions**
Did you work hard?	Didn't you work hard?
Answers	**Negative answers**
Yes, I did	No, I didn't

Spelling notes

You add *-ed* or *-d* to the base form of the verb to form the past tense of regular verbs:

work – worked, like – liked, change – changed, pull – pulled, seem – seemed, stamp – stamped

Some verbs which end in a vowel (*-a*, *-e*, *-i*, *-o* or *-u*) and a consonant, double the consonant for the past tense form:

stop – stopped, beg – begged, plan – planned, pin – pinned

Verbs which end in a consonant + *-y*, use *-ied* for the past tense form:

carry – carried, try – tried, rely – relied

but when a verb ends in a vowel + *-y*, the past tense form is *-yed*:

obey – obeyed, play – played, annoy – annoyed

Present Continuous Tense

I'm listening to this play on the radio.

You use the present continuous tense to talk about:

something which is happening now, at the time of speaking:

Look at the baby! He's trying to climb onto the chair.
Why are you sitting here in the dark?
I'm listening to this play on the radio.
Shall we clear up while they're eating their supper?
That smells good. What are you cooking?

something which is happening for a limited period of time in the present, but perhaps not at the time of speaking:

I'm learning to play golf. I'm taking lessons.
I'm reading a really good book. Would you like to borrow it when I've finished it?
My wife's working in Manchester for a few weeks.
They're building some new houses at the end of the road.

You can use the present continuous to talk about the future, when you have a definite arrangement or plan:

We're meeting outside the Odeon at 6 this evening.
They're leaving next Thursday.
Are you coming to the pub with us after work? No, sorry, I can't. I'm meeting my husband and we're going to the cinema.
What are you doing next Friday?

Form

Positive	Negative
I am coming	I am not coming
You are coming	You are not coming
He/she/it is coming	He/she/it is not coming
We are coming	We are not coming
You are coming	You are not coming
They are coming	They are not coming

Short forms

I'm coming	I'm not coming
You're coming	You're not/you aren't coming
He's/she's/it's coming	He's/she's/it's not coming He/she/it isn't coming
We're coming	We're not/we aren't coming
You're coming	You're not/you aren't coming
They're coming	They're not/they aren't coming

Questions	Negative questions
Are you coming?	Aren't you coming?

Answers	Negative answers
Yes, I am	No, I'm not

Spelling notes

Verbs which end in a single *-e*, drop the *-e* before the *-ing*:
make – making, shape – shaping, argue – arguing

Verbs which end in a vowel and a single consonant, double the consonant before the *-ing*:
sit – sitting, plan – planning, stop – stopping, travel – travelling, signal – signalling

Usage note

Some verbs are not used in the continuous forms. See the notes on page 24 for a list of these verbs.

Past Continuous Tense

He **was working** in the garden at the weekend.

You use the past continuous tense:

to talk about an activity that happened for some time in the past. We don't say when it started or when it finished:

While we were waiting for the ambulance to come, everyone was rushing around trying to help.
When I arrived, several people were sitting near the window talking.
He was working in the garden at the weekend.

to describe a scene in a story:

We knew something was wrong. People were whispering to one another and others were getting up and leaving.
When they set off, the sun was already shining.

to describe what was happening at a particular time in the past:

It was still raining at 7 o'clock this morning.

Usage note

When something happens during a longer activity, or interrupts it, you use the past continuous tense for the longer, incomplete activity and the past simple tense for the shorter, completed activity:

We were standing at the bus stop when I noticed the blue car stop.
I was talking to Jean the other day and she told me about your job.
I was watching TV at 8 o'clock when the bomb exploded.
He phoned me while I was still having breakfast.

Form

Positive

I was waiting
You were waiting
He/she/it was waiting
We were waiting
You were waiting
They were waiting

Negative

I was not waiting
You were not waiting
He/she/it was not waiting
We were not waiting
You were not waiting
They were not waiting

Short forms

I wasn't waiting
You weren't waiting
He/she/it wasn't waiting
We weren't waiting
You weren't waiting
They weren't waiting

Questions

Were you waiting?

Negative questions

Weren't you waiting?

Answers

Yes, I was

Negative answers

No, I wasn't

Spelling notes

Verbs which end in a single *-e*, drop the *-e* before the *-ing*:

make – making, shape – shaping, argue – arguing

Verbs which end in a vowel and a single consonant, double the consonant before the *-ing*:

sit – sitting, plan – planning, stop – stopping, travel – travelling, signal – signalling

Usage note

Some verbs are not used in the continuous forms. See the notes on page 24 for a list of these verbs.

Compare the present simple and the present continuous

Some verbs are not used in the continuous tenses. These include:

Verbs like *be*: appear, seem
I am happy.
She seems a nice person.

Verbs like *know*: think, believe, agree, understand, remember, forget, imagine, mean, realise, recognise, suppose, trust
I know a lot about business matters.
He believes that he will win the election.

Verbs like *see*: feel, hear, smell, sound, taste, notice, observe
I smell smoke.
I think I hear a bell.

Verbs like *like*: want, wish, love, hate, dislike, prefer, surprise, impress, please, loathe, mind, adore, appreciate, care, desire, detest, fear
I like this film a lot.
She wants a bicycle very much.

Verbs like *have*: own, belong to, contain, include, need, owe, possess
They have their own house now.
She owns three cars.

Verbs like *cost*: weigh
This coat costs £65.
That steak weighs 1.5 kilos.

Usage note

You can use *can* with verbs like *see* to give a meaning like the continuous:
I can smell smoke.
I think I can hear a bell.

Compare the past simple and the past continuous tenses:

Lila lived in Calcutta for twenty years. (past simple)
Ali was living in Paris for a year. (past continuous)

You use the past simple tense to show a permanent situation and the past continuous tense to show a temporary one. So we understand that Lila's home was in Calcutta and her family, job or school were there. We understand that Ali went to Paris for a holiday or visit or a short course of studies. Usually, the permanent state lasts longer than the temporary state.

Pete taught himself Arabic. (past simple)
Bill was teaching himself Arabic. (past continuous)

You use the past simple tense to show that an action was completed, so we know that Pete succeeded in learning Arabic. You use the past continuous tense for an action when you do not know when it finished or if it was completed. So we don't know if Bill was successful in learning Arabic or not.

Everyone at the ceremony wore formal dress. (past simple)
The King was wearing military costume. (past continuous)

You use the past simple tense most frequently to talk about events or actions that happened in the past. But you use the past continuous tense for descriptions and stories.

The baby jumped up and down when he saw his mother. (past simple)
The boy was jumping up and down when he saw his mother. (past continuous)

You use the past simple tense for short, sudden actions. So the baby saw his mother first, then jumped up and down as a result of seeing her. You use the past continuous tense for longer actions when you do not say when they began or ended. So the boy was already jumping when he noticed his mother.

Present Perfect Tense

The bus **has** just **left**.

The present perfect tense links past and present time. Use this tense to talk about:

something which happened very recently in the past, often just a few minutes before, and which is still important in the present:

The bus has just left.
That's a shame! You've just missed him.
He's gone to the station to pick up his mother. He'll be back in a minute.
I think I've broken my leg. I can't stand on it.

NOTE that you can use *just* to emphasise that the action happened very recently.

something which happened recently in the past. We don't say when it happened, but it is still important in the present:

Would you like something to eat? No thanks, I've already had my dinner.
They've reached the summit but I haven't heard if they have started the descent yet.
Look, I've shampooed the carpet. Doesn't it look nice?

something which began in the past, and which is still true right up to the present time:

We've been here all day but nobody has rung.
I haven't played hockey for ages – not for three months or more.
It has only rained once during the last month.
They have lived in Jamaica since 1982.

NOTE that we often use words and phrases like *all morning*, *all day*, *all this afternoon/month*, *all my life*, *during the last few weeks/years*, *so far*, *recently*, *lately*, *for* and *since* in this meaning.

something which happened recently, and which is not yet finished:

I've written three letters today and I've still got two more to do.
Have you seen the news today? No, I haven't had a chance yet.

NOTE that we often use words and phrases like *this morning/afternoon/week/month/year* and *today* in this meaning.

You use it for asking people questions about experiences which are true for both the past and the present, and for telling people about experiences in general:

Have you ever eaten Japanese food? – No, I haven't.
Has she ever been to India? – Yes, I think she has.
Have you seen the new Woody Allen film? – Not yet.
I've never been skiing.
They have never met their real parents.

NOTE that we often use words like *ever*, *never*, *before*, *already* and *yet* in this meaning.

Usage note

As soon as you mention a particular time in the past (*a few minutes ago, at 10 o'clock, yesterday, on Thursday, then, when, as, last week, in July*), you must use the past simple tense to talk about a past action, however recent it was:

Have they arrived yet? Yes, they got there at 7.30.
The President has been killed. He was shot as he left the Parliament building.
Have they been told yet? – Yes, I spoke to them an hour ago.

Form

Positive	Negative
I have changed	I have not changed
You have changed	You have not changed
He/she/it has changed	He/she/it has not changed
We have changed	We have not changed
You have changed	You have not changed
They have changed	They have not changed
Short forms	
I've changed	I haven't changed
You've changed	You haven't changed
He's/she's/it's changed	He/she/it hasn't changed
We've changed	We haven't changed
You've changed	You haven't changed
They've changed	They haven't changed
Questions	**Negative questions**
Have you changed?	Haven't you changed?
Answers	**Negative answers**
Yes, I have	No, I haven't

Spelling notes

You add *-ed* or *-d* to the base form of the verb to form the past participle of regular verbs:

work – worked, like – liked, stamp – stamped, pull – pulled

Some verbs which end in a vowel (*-a*, *-e*, *-i*, *-o* or *-u*) and a consonant, double the consonant for the past participle form:

stop – stopped, beg – begged, plan – planned

Verbs which end in a consonant + *-y*, use *-ied* for the past participle form:

carry – carried, try – tried, supply – supplied

but when a verb ends in a vowel + *-y*, the form is *-yed*:

obey – obeyed, play – played, annoy – annoyed

Check the past participle of irregular verbs from the list at the back of this book (page 131).

Compare the present perfect and past simple tenses

Mr Barrow has lived in that house for 20 years.
(present perfect)
John Parker lived in Borneo for 15 years.
(past simple)

You use the present perfect tense to talk about something which was true in the past and which is still true in the present, but you must use the past simple tense when something was true only in the past and is finished now. So we understand from the first sentence that Mr Barrow still lives in that same house which he moved into 20 years ago. But we know from the second sentence that John Parker does not live in Borneo now; he spent 15 years there but he left at some time in the past.

Look, Linda has painted the kitchen. (present perfect)
Peter painted the bathroom bright blue. (past simple)

You use the present perfect tense when you are interested in the present result of a past action, even when that action happened a long time ago. So Linda may have painted the kitchen months ago or only a week ago, but you are showing it to someone who has not seen it since it was changed: the present, new state of the kitchen is important. When you tell someone a simple fact, a past action, you use the past simple tense. So we know that Peter (not any other person) painted the bathroom and that he painted it blue (not yellow or another colour).

Meryl Streep has won two Oscars. (present perfect)
She won her first Oscar for 'Kramer v. Kramer'. (past simple)

You use the present perfect tense when you are not interested in when something happened. You are interested in any time up to the present, that is, general experience. So we are thinking of the whole of Meryl Streep's film career and her achievements. You use the past simple tense to talk about a particular experience in the past, for example, when Meryl Streep made one film, 'Kramer v. Kramer', and won an award for it.

Present Perfect Continuous Tense

John **has been learning** to play the piano for two years now.

You use the present perfect continuous tense:

to talk about an action which began in the past and has continued without stopping up to the present. So the action is not yet finished:

John has been learning to play the piano for two years now.
I have been going into Stockport to do my shopping every week since we moved here.

to talk about an action which began in the past and continued without stopping up to a few moments ago. So the action has only just finished:

I'm exhausted! I've been working in the garage all day.
Have you been running? You sound out of breath.

Usage notes

You use the present perfect continuous tense when you want to stress the importance of an activity, and the present perfect tense when you want to stress the result of the activity:

I've been writing letters all morning. (the activity)
I've written five letters this morning. (the result)

You use the present perfect continuous tense when you want to show the importance of something happening, and the present perfect tense when you want to show the importance of something staying the same:

Bob Brown has been running that garage for 10 years.
Mr King has managed the Renault factory for 5 years.

Some verbs are not used in the continuous forms. See the notes on page 24 for a list of these verbs.

Form

Positive	**Negative**
I have been working	I have not been working
You have been working	You have not been working
He/she/it has been working	He/she/it has not been working
We have been working	We have not been working
You have been working	You have not been working
They have been working	They have not been working
Short forms	
I've been working	I haven't been working
You've been working	You haven't been working
He's/she's/it's been working	He/she/it hasn't been working
We've been working	We haven't been working
You've been working	You haven't been working
They've been working	They haven't been working
Questions	**Negative questions**
Have you been working?	Haven't you been working?
Answers	**Negative answers**
Yes, I have	No, I haven't

The present perfect with *for* and *since*

You use *for* and *since* when you talk about something which started in the past and has continued up to the present time and is still true:

We have lived in York for 20 years, since we got married.
They have only known each other for a few weeks.

You use *for* with a period of time to talk about how long something lasted:

for a few minutes/two hours/three days/a week/
the last few months/several years/ages/
a long time/as long as I can remember

NOTE **that you can often omit *for* when you speak or write.**

You use *since* with a point in time (a time, a date, etc.) to say when something started. You cannot omit *since* when you speak or write.

since half past three/ten o'clock/midnight/
last week/last month/Tuesday/the end of July/
23rd March/Christmas/1982/my birthday

Past Perfect Tense

> After we **had finished** our meal, we paid the bill and left.

You use the past perfect tense:

when you want to show that two things happened at different times, both of them in the past. You use the past perfect tense for the action which happened first, and the simple past tense for the action which happened later:

After we had finished our meal, we paid the bill and left.
No one had ever seen him before. He just arrived one day.
I couldn't phone you because I'd left your number behind.
They decided to go home when they'd done all the work.
Sue didn't come with us. She'd already arranged to meet Jim.

Past Perfect Continuous Tense

> They **had been walking** all day when they reached the pub.

You can also use the past perfect continuous tense to show that two things happened at different times in the past. But you use it when you want to stress that something was happening for a long time and was still continuing or had only just stopped when the second, later action happened:

They had been walking all day when they reached the pub.
He'd been lying there for some time before we found him.

Form

Past perfect tense

Positive	**Negative**
I had seen it	I had not seen it
You had seen it	You had not seen it
He/she/it had seen it	He/she/it had not seen it
We had seen it	We had not seen it
You had seen it	You had not seen it
They had seen it	They had not seen it
Short forms	
I'd seen it	I hadn't seen it
You'd seen it	You hadn't seen it
He'd/she'd/it'd seen it	He/she/it hadn't seen it
We'd seen it	We hadn't seen it
You'd seen it	You hadn't seen it
They'd seen it	They hadn't seen it
Questions	**Negative questions**
Had you seen it?	Hadn't you seen it?
Answers	**Negative answers**
Yes, I had	No, I hadn't

Past perfect continuous tense

Positive	**Negative**
I had been walking	I had not been walking
Short forms	
I'd been walking	I hadn't been walking
Questions	**Negative questions**
Had you been walking?	Hadn't you been walking?
Answers	**Negative answers**
Yes, I had	No, I hadn't

Usage note

Some verbs are not used in the continuous forms. See the notes on page 24 for a list of these verbs.

Future Tenses

When **will** you **start** your new job?

You use *will* to talk about the future:

when something is certain to happen (or not happen):

Student registration will take place on 1st June.
There won't be any money left for a party this year.
Your new flat won't be ready until the end of March.
When will you start your new job?

when you have just decided to do something, or offered to do something, or when you ask someone to do something for you. You always make this decision, offer or request at the time of speaking:

Is that someone at the door? – I'll go and see.
I think I'll ask Charles to come with us tonight.
What would you like to drink? – I'll have a gin and bitter lemon, please.
This box is terribly heavy. – We'll carry it for you.
I can't do this problem! – Jane'll help you, she's good at maths.
Will you post this letter for me while you're out?

when you say what you think or feel about the future, although you cannot be sure that it will actually happen. You are predicting the future.

Do you think it will rain tonight?
I don't suppose they'll remember to bring the photos.
We know you'll do well in your exams! – No, I won't!
Things will get better. You wait and see!
Don't worry. Perhaps you'll hear from him tomorrow.

NOTE that we often use words and phrases like *think*, *know*, *believe*, *suppose*, *hope*, *feel sure*, *wonder*, *doubt*, *probably* and *perhaps* in this use.

Form

Positive	**Negative**
I will go	I will not go
You will go	You will not go
He/she/it will go	He/she/it will not go
We will go	We will not go
You will go	You will not go
They will go	They will not go
Short forms	
I'll go	I won't go
You'll go	You won't go
He'll/she'll/it'll go	He/she/it won't go
We'll go	We won't go
You'll go	You won't go
They'll go	They won't go
Questions	**Negative questions**
Will you go?	Won't you go?
Answers	**Negative answers**
Yes, I will	No, I won't

Usage notes

You can use *shall/shan't* instead of *will/won't* in some cases, but only with the *I* and *we* forms:

You can use *shall/shan't* to state a fact:

We shall be in Tokyo this time next week.
I shan't see you again before you go.

You can use *shall* in questions, when you offer to do something for someone, and for suggestions:

What shall I do?
When shall we go to the Louvre?
Shall I bring the menu now?
Shall we go and see Sarah this evening?

She's **going to** have a baby.

You use *be going to* to talk about the future:

when something has been planned or decided on. You can be sure that the action will happen because it is prepared:

We're going to visit our son in Canada in August: we're really looking forward to it.
What's he going to do when he finishes school? He's going to study medicine.
I'm going to ask for a rise. I'm fed up with my low pay!
She's going to have a baby.

when you say that an event will happen because you can see clearly that it will happen. Again, you are sure it will happen:

Look at those dark clouds! It's going to snow tonight.
Look out! That lorry's going to crash!
She isn't going to pass her exams: she's hardly done any work since Christmas.
She's going to have a baby.

Usage note

You can use the past form of *be going to* to talk about past plans and predictions:

I was going to start a new job in July but I went into hospital so I still haven't started it.
They were going to phone me when they heard any news.
We knew there was going to be trouble because all the men were standing around looking angry.

Look at p:20 for the use of the present continuous as a future.

Form

Positive	Negative
I am going to eat	I am not going to eat
You are going to eat	You are not going to eat
He/she/it is going to eat	He/she/it is not going to eat
We are going to eat	We are not going to eat
You are going to eat	You are not going to eat
They are going to eat	They are not going to eat
Short forms	
I'm going to eat	I'm not going to eat
You're going to eat	You aren't going to eat
He's/she's/it's going to eat	He/she/it isn't going to eat
We're going to eat	We aren't going to eat
You're going to eat	You aren't going to eat
They're going to eat	They aren't going to eat
Questions	**Negative questions**
Are you going to eat?	Aren't you going to eat?
Answers	**Negative answers**
Yes, I am	No, I'm not

Usage notes

You can use *be about to* to talk about the very near future; about something which will happen in the next few minutes or seconds:

Please take your seats! The show is about to start.
Don't leave yet. It's just about to stop raining.
I was just about to give up when I noticed my keys lying on the floor in a corner.

You can use *be to* to give information about future arrangements. This is very formal and is used only in written English:

The President is to appear on television tomorrow.
The leaders are to meet again in two months.

Future Continuous Tense

The mayor **will be talking** about local issues all day tomorrow.

You use the future continuous tense to talk about:

something which will happen during a time in the future:

The mayor will be talking about local issues all day tomorrow.
I expect they'll be staying in London for some time.

something which is fairly certain to happen in the future:

You don't need to phone. I'll be seeing him tomorrow.
A new 'Dallas' series will be starting on BBC1 in the autumn.

Future Perfect Tense

The decorators **will have finished** painting by next week.

You use the future perfect tense to say that something will be finished (or not finished) by a certain time in the future:

The decorators will have finished painting by next week.
I can't come at 7: I won't have finished my dinner then.

Usage note

You can use the future perfect continuous tense when you want to show that something has been happening for a long period of time:

In July, Harry *will have been working* here for 15 years.

Form

Future continuous tense

I will be staying	I will not be staying
You will be staying	You will not be staying
He/she/it will be staying	He/she/it will not be staying
We will be staying	We will not be staying
You will be staying	You will not be staying
They will be staying	They will not be staying

Short forms

I'll be staying	I won't be staying
You'll be staying	You won't be staying
He'll/she'll/it'll be staying	He/she/it won't be staying
We'll be staying	We won't be staying
You'll be staying	You won't be staying
They'll be staying	They won't be staying

Questions	**Negative questions**
Will you be staying?	Won't you be staying?

Answers	**Negative answers**
Yes, I will	No, I won't

Future perfect tense

I will have finished	I will not have finished

Short forms

I'll have finished	I won't have finished

Questions

Will you have finished?	Won't you have finished?

Answers

Yes, I will	No, I won't

Future perfect continuous tense

I will have been working	I will not have been working

Usage note

Some verbs are not used in the continuous forms. See the notes on page 24 for a list of these verbs.

Conditional Sentences

If he **works** hard, he**'ll pass** his exams.

You use conditional sentences to show what would happen if something was true. Conditional sentences have two clauses, and one of them always starts with *if*. You can use the *if*-clause first or second, it doesn't matter.

There are four main types of conditional sentences, and they all mean slightly different things. We show you each type in the next few pages.

If you **mix** red and white, you **get** pink.

You use this type of sentence to talk about something which is always true at any time in the past, present or future. Whenever the first condition happens (you mix red and white together) then the other event will also happen (you get pink).

The condition may be true for everyone, or for just one person or one particular situation:

If the temperature falls, the boiler switches on automatically.
If I get very tired, my back starts aching.
If I'm working very hard, I never notice the time.
The bus is always very crowded if it comes late.
We don't let any more people in if it gets very busy.

Usage note

In this type of general conditional sentence, you can replace *if* with *when*:

I never notice the time when I'm working very hard.

If Peter **works** hard this year, he **will pass** his exams.

You use this type of sentence when you think it is quite possible for something to happen now or in the future. You do not know for certain if Peter will work hard or not, but if he does then you know he will pass his exams. Other examples of real conditions are:

If I have enough money next year, I'll go to China.
If he doesn't hurry up, he'll lose his place.
If you ask at the desk, someone will tell you where to go.
That dog will bite you if you touch it.
Mrs Patel won't come if the weather turns bad.
Will I be there in time if I go now? – Yes, probably.
Do you think Peter will pass his exams if he works hard? – Yes, I expect so.

Usage notes

You can use other modal verbs like *can*, *might*, *should* and *ought to* instead of *will*:

If he works hard, he might pass his exams.
If you have enough time, you should go to China.
They can always ask if they have any difficulties.

You can change the present simple tense in the *if*-clause to the present perfect tense, the present continuous tense or a modal verb:

If you've never eaten Japanese food, you should try some now.
If he's been to a tropical country, he'll know what I mean.
If she is studying hard, she won't have time to come.
Will you call in and see us if you're passing by?
If we can do anything, we will always be pleased to help out.
If they can't find it, what should they do?

You can use the imperative form to give instructions and advice:

If it's too difficult, don't worry. Just leave it.
If it starts raining, remember to take your umbrella.
Close all the windows if you're going out all day.
If there's anything we can do, please ask.

If I won the football pools, I would sail round the world.

You use this type of sentence:

when you expect something not to happen, in the present or future, even though it is possible. This is an unreal condition:

If we lived in the country, we could have a big garden and grow our own vegetables.
(We don't live in the country, but if we did . . .)
If Peter worked harder, he would pass his exams.
(You don't expect Peter to work harder, but if he did . . .)
You'd feel much better if you didn't smoke so much.
You wouldn't recognise Jenny now even if you bumped into her in the street. She has changed so much!
What would you do if you saw someone shoplifting? – Well, I don't think I would go up to them. I'd go and find a shop assistant and tell them.

to talk about something which is impossible in the present, and quite different from the real facts:

If we were rich, we could buy our own shop.
If he could speak French, it would be much easier.
If I still had my car, I'd take you to Chester myself.
He'd be much happier if he worked for himself.

to talk in a polite, not very definite, way about future plans:

Would you be interested in coming if I arranged the transport? – Yes, I would.
If we saved at least £50 a month until next March, we might be able to afford to go.

to give advice to someone, using *If I were you . . .*:

If I were you, I'd go and see the doctor about that rash.
I'd find out about it as soon as possible if I were you.

NOTE that you are not talking about the past even though you use the past simple tense in the *if*-clause.

If Charlie **had phoned** me, I **would have come** at once.

You use this type of sentence:

to talk about past situations which did not happen. Charlie did not phone me so I did not come. Other examples of unreal past conditions are:

If we had had more money, we could have bought more presents in China.
(We didn't have much money so we couldn't buy many presents.)
We were lucky! If it had rained yesterday they would have cancelled the match.
(It didn't rain so the match wasn't cancelled.)
We would have been there on time if the bus had come.
Would you have gone if they'd asked you?
I might have been able to finish if there'd been more time.

to talk about situations which were impossible in the past:

I'd have warned you myself if I had known.
(I didn't know so I couldn't warn you.)
He wouldn't have done it even if you'd been here to help him.

Usage note

You can use the past perfect continuous tense in the *if*-clause to talk about an activity which continued for a long time in the past:

If he'd been wearing his safety belt, he wouldn't have been killed.
If we'd been sitting near the front we'd have enjoyed the play more.

Imperatives

Come and **join** us! **Don't sit** over there on your own!

You use the imperative:

to order someone to do something:

Hurry up now children! We'll all be late.
Take this order down to the print room, please, and then come back here.
Don't tell anyone about this!

to warn someone about a danger or a possible problem:

Be careful! The road is very slippery here.
Don't forget. The film starts at 8.15 so we must be there at 7.30 to be sure of a seat.

to give instructions and to explain how to do something:

Mix the flour and sugar together first and then add two spoons of warm water.
Turn left at the corner and take the third right.
Take one tablet three times a day after meals.

to make offers and invitations:

Come in and have a drink with us!
If there's anything I can do, don't hesitate to ask.
Please help yourselves.

for instructions and warnings on written signs and notices:

Lift the receiver and listen to the dialling tone.
Insert 10p.
Do not leave clothes in the changing rooms. Use the lockers.

Form

You use the base form of the verb as the imperative. The form is the same whether you are speaking to one person or to more than one person.

You use *don't* in front of the base form of the verb to make a negative imperative.

Usage notes

You can add *do* to an imperative for emphasis. It can show special persuasion or irritation:

Do be quieter boys! Granny's trying to rest.
Do hurry up! How many times must I tell you?

You can use a noun or pronoun with the imperative to make it clear who you are talking to:

Anna sit down.
You boys come here.

You can use *let's* to include yourself in the order. This makes it seem more like a suggestion than a command:

Let's wait for Nick. I don't want to miss him.
Don't let's tell Shirley yet. We'll make it a surprise.

The negative form of *let's* is either *let's not* or *don't let's. Let's not* is more formal:

Don't let's argue about it again!
Let's not wait for David any longer.

Active and Passive

The Romans built this wall/This wall was built by the Romans.

In English, new or important information is usually put at the end of a sentence. The active sentence *The Romans built this wall* means that 'the wall' is new information, while the passive sentence *This wall was built by the Romans* means that 'the Romans' is new information.

You use the passive:

when you want to make the subject of an active sentence the new information:

The lights are switched off at 10.30 by the nurse.
This beautiful picture was painted by Renoir.
The Globe theatre will be opened by the new director.
The Olympic Games were watched by 50 million viewers.

or when it is not necessary to say who the subject of the active sentence is at all. This may be because it is very obvious who the subject is:

A man is being questioned about yesterday's bank raid.
(The police are questioning a man about . . .)
Your new table will be delivered on Thursday.
(The shop will deliver your new table . . .)
This book should be returned by 3 November.
(You should return this book by . . .)

or because it is not important to mention the subject:

Breakfast is served every morning between 8 and 9.30.
These jeans were made in South Korea.

or because we do not know who the subject is:

My car was stolen last week.
Look! That window has been broken.

Form

Positive	Negative
Present simple tense	
I am allowed to drink	I am not allowed to drink
Past simple tense	
I was given a bike	I was not given a bike
Present continuous tense	
I am being met by Anna	I am not being met by Anna
Past continuous tense	
I was being helped by Peter	I was not being helped by Peter
Present perfect tense	
I have been asked to speak	I have not been asked to speak
Past perfect tense	
I had been asked to stay	I had not been asked to stay
Future	
I will be told tomorrow	I will not be told tomorrow
Future perfect tense	
It will have been done by Friday	It will not have been done by Friday

Check the past participle of irregular verbs from the list at the back of this book (page 131).

Usage note

These passive tenses follow the same patterns as the active tenses. Look at the sections on the active verbs for full examples of the different forms and their uses.

A lot of people **got left** behind when the train went.

You can use the verb *get* to form the passive instead of *be*:

to show that something happens and that it is not a permanent state. It has the same meaning as *become*:

I get annoyed when people keep talking in the cinema.
They got so bored with the talk that they went home.
A lot of people got left behind when the train went.

to show when something happens by accident:

This shirt got torn in the washing machine.
How did the garage door get damaged?
I got soaked on my way home tonight in that storm.

in some common expressions which describe what you do or what happens to you:

I always get washed and dressed before I make my tea in the morning.
They got married last week without telling anyone.
How did you get lost? I thought you knew the way.

I **had** my hair **cut** this morning.

You can use *have/get something done* when you ask someone to do something for you. You use this form of the passive when another person performs a service for you, for example, a hairdresser who cuts your hair, a mechanic who repairs your car or a decorator who paints your house:

I had my hair cut this morning. Do you like it?
I'm getting the car serviced next week. It's not running very well.
Have you had your house painted? It looks very smart.
Where can you have your suit dry-cleaned near here?
I've got toothache. I must have my teeth checked.

Modal Verbs

I **might** come with you. I **will** tell you tonight.

The modal verbs are:

can, could, may, might, shall, should, will, would, must, ought to, need, dare, used to.

Modal verbs are always used with another verb in a sentence, to change its meaning in some way. They often show the mood or attitude of the speaker.

You use these verbs with a main verb in a sentence. You always put the main verb (an infinitive without *to*) after the modal verb:

I might come; I can let you know tonight.
You ought to phone your mother. She must be worried.

The modal verbs do not have *-s*, *-ing*, or *-ed* forms. *Can*, *may*, *shall* and *will* have special past forms *could*, *might*, *should* and *would*:

I could swim when I was five.
He said he would get in touch.

You always put the negative *not* or *n't* after the modal verb and before the main verb:

You must not leave the windows open.
I dare not tell them the whole truth.
It shouldn't be difficult to find the way.

You always put the modal verb before the subject when you make a question:

Can I help you?
Will they phone us and let us know?

You use the modal verbs to talk about:

what is possible and not possible:
may, might, can, could

what is necessary and not necessary:
must, (have to), (have got to), need to, needn't, should ought to

someone's ability to do something:
can, could, (be able to)

your intention to do something:
will, would

permission, including asking for and giving it:
can, could, may, might, (be allowed to)

to give advice and make suggestions:
should, can, could, shall

to make offers and requests:
can, could, shall

to talk about the future:
will, shall, would

to talk about the past:
used to, would

to talk about imaginary situations:
would

to talk about obligation:
must, ought to, should, have got to, need

to talk about certainty/likelihood:
will, must, can't, should

to mean be brave enough:
dare

Can

Can he speak Spanish? – Yes, he **can.**

You use the modal verb *can* to talk about:

what you know how to do, or are able to do, either all the time or at one time in a particular situation:

Can he speak Spanish? – Yes, he can.
I'm sorry, I can't help you. I can't drive, you see.
Can you read that sign up there? It isn't very clear.

having, asking and giving permission to do something:

I can borrow my Dad's car to go to the dance tonight!
Can I use your phone please? – Yes, certainly.
You can go and play over the park for an hour, if you like.

the possibility of doing something. It doesn't matter whether you actually do it or not:

You could walk here until they built the new road.
You can park round the back of the town hall if the big car park is full.
You can't camp here. It isn't safe.
Can you see the mountains from the hotel?
Anyone can phone and speak to the manager.

and the possibility of something happening occasionally:

This beach can be dangerous when the sea is rough.
(Sometimes this beach is dangerous.)
The river can flood in a very wet year.
(It is possible for the river to flood, but it only happens sometimes.)
Joe can be very bad-tempered when he's busy.

In all of these uses, *could* is the past form of *can*.

You can also use *can* to offer to help other people and to ask other people to help you.

Can I get you something to eat?
Can you close the window, it's getting cold?

NOTE that *could* is not the past form of *can* for this use.

Usage notes

When you are sure that something is impossible, you use *can't* + infinitive to talk about the present and *can't have* + past participle for the past:

You can't still be hungry. We've only just had dinner.
They can't have gone home. Their coats are still here.

NOTE that you can use *couldn't* for the past with the same meaning.

Tom couldn't have done all that work on his own. He doesn't know enough about engineering.

You can use *be able to* instead of *can* when you want to talk about ability in the future:

We'll be able to meet you at the airport next Tuesday.
You should be able to see a baseball match while you're in Texas. I'll try and get a ticket for you.
All children ought to be able to read by the time they are seven.

You can also use *be allowed to* to talk about having permission, especially official permission, or refusal which is given by the police or other authorities:

You aren't allowed to walk on the grass in this park.
He was allowed to leave the country after some delay.
Are we allowed to borrow these books? – Yes, you can take up to three at one time.

Could

My sister could swim when she was only three years old.

You use the modal verb *could* as the past tense of *can* to talk about:

what you knew how to do, or were able to do, in the past:

We couldn't open the door. The lock was very stiff.
My sister could swim when she was only three years old.

having permission to do something in the past:

We could go into town on Saturday afternoons but we had to be back at school by 5 o'clock.

the possibility of doing something in the past. It doesn't matter whether you actually did it or not:

You could walk here until they built the new road.

and the possibility of something happening occasionally in the past:

Joe could be very bad-tempered when he was a baby.

Usage notes

You also use *could* to ask for permission to do something in the present or future. It is more formal than *can*:

Could we bring our nephew with us? – Yes, of course you can.

When the possibility is very uncertain and you do not know the true facts, you use *could* + infinitive for the present and *could have* + past participle for the past to suggest a possible explanation:

What's happened to Harry? He's very late. – He could still be at work. – Yes, he could be, or his car could've broken down.

When something was possible in the past, but did not actually happen, you use *could have* + past participle:

You were stupid to go on that ice – you could have fallen in.

May/Might

I **may** be able to help you.

You use the modal verbs *may* and *might* to:

talk about the possibility of something happening in the present or in the future. *Might* is a little less sure or certain than *may*:

I may be able to help you.
(It is possible that I can help you but not certain.)
Your car might be ready by Saturday.
(Perhaps your car will be ready but we are not sure.)
The shop might not be open today.
(It's a holiday so the shop is likely to be closed.)
We may see you there, if we decide to go.

ask permission in a fairly formal way. *May* is more common than *might* and you will also see *may* used to give or refuse permission in a formal, often official, way:

May I borrow your calculator for a minute, please?
Students may not have visitors in their rooms.

Usage notes

You use *might* instead of *may* when you report a possibility in the past tense:

He said he might join us later on.
We knew she might die.

You use *Do you think?* or *Is it likely?* + *will* to ask questions about possibility:

Do you think you'll be able to help me?
Is it likely that the car will be ready by Saturday?
or: Is the car likely to be ready by Saturday?
When do you think they'll come?

You use *may/might have* + past participle to talk about the possibility that something happened in the past. You do not know for certain if it happened or not:

I might have left my case at the office.
(I can't find my case – perhaps I left it at work.)
It's odd that he hasn't come. He may have got lost.
(We don't know where he is – it is possible that he lost his way.)
He might not have remembered our meeting.

You use *might have* + past participle when a past event was possible, but you know it did not actually happen:

You were stupid to drink that water. It might have been poisonous.
We should have taken the coast road. We might have got there earlier.

Will

Maria will be 21 years old next week.

You use *will* (negative: *will not*/*won't*):

to talk about the future:

Maria will be 21 years old next week.
We'll be in Rome this time tomorrow.
I won't be able to play in the match on Saturday.

to talk about what you intend or decide to do:

I'll take the red pair I think.
That'll be Mike at the door. I'll let him in.

to talk about what you promise, agree, offer or refuse to do:

We will do all we can to sort out your problem.
I promise I'll come back as soon as I can.
We'll give you a lift to the station.
I'll do the washing-up. You sit down and have a rest.
He won't let me go to Angie's party.
My car won't start. I don't know what's wrong with it.
You must eat your dinner up! – No, I won't!

to talk about what is certain or likely to be the case:

If you leave now, you'll probably catch the train.
I don't expect it'll arrive today.

NOTE **that if you use a past tense verb in these uses, then you use *would* instead of *will*.**

to ask someone to do something:

Will you help me move this box over there, please?
Will you give this to Maggie when you see her?
Will you sit here, please?

Would

They said they **would** be here by 4 o'clock.

You use *would*:

as the past of *will* when you talk about a past event. *Wouldn't* becomes the past of *won't*:

They said they would be here by 4 o'clock.
She was upset because they wouldn't let her see him.

when you ask or invite someone to do something, and offer something, *would* is politer than *will*:

Would you wait here for a minute, please?
Would you mind closing the door after you?
Would you like another cup of coffee? – No, thank you.

Usage notes

You use *would* to talk about imaginary situations which do not exist (yet):

If I had time I'd go and see the new exhibition.
It would be great if Liverpool won the Cup!

You use *would* to wish for something, after *I wish* and *If only* and with other verbs of wishing or liking. These also talk about imaginary situations:

I wish they would go away!
If only it would get warmer.
She would like to be able to paint really well.

We use *would rather* to show a preference for one thing:

Would you rather have tea or coffee?
She'd rather work in a shop than an office.
We would prefer to go at the weekend.

Shall

We shall be away for two weeks.

You use *shall*:

with *I/we* for the future form instead of *will* or *won't*:

I expect I shall see you later on.
We shall be away for two weeks.
I shan't come if they don't provide some transport.
We shall win the fight against crime!

to offer to do something:

Shall I ask if there are any more tickets?
Shall we stop at your place on our way and see if you need a lift? – Yes, if you don't mind.
Shall I finish the clearing up? – Yes, thanks a lot.

to make suggestions:

Shall we go for a drive this afternoon?
Shall I take her to see the new shopping centre?
Let's see if Martin can come, shall we?

to ask for advice or help about what to do:

What shall I do with all these empty boxes?
Where shall we go today?
How shall I cook this fish?

NOTE that *shan't* is the short form of *shall not*.

Should

We **should** eat more fresh vegetables.

You use *should*:

to talk about what you think is the right thing to do or the correct situation to exist:

We should eat more fresh vegetables.
He shouldn't smoke so much.
I should speak to Lucy about it: she always knows what to do.
That should be all right. There's plenty of time.

sometimes this means giving advice about the best thing to do:

He should see a doctor if his cold doesn't get better.
I should go, if I were you.

to ask other people for their advice or opinion on the right thing to do:

What should I do about it?
How much do you think we should ask for?
Should I go, d'you think?

to talk about what is likely to happen:

The children should be home soon. They left school an hour ago.

to make offers and suggestions:

Should I lay the table for supper yet?
Should I see if there's anything on TV?

Usage note

You can use *should* + *have* + past participle to talk about past correct actions or obligations which someone did not do:

She is very upset: someone should have helped her.
I feel awful. I shouldn't have eaten so many sweets.

Ought to

He ought to change his job if he's not happy there.

You can use *ought to* just like *should*:

to talk about what you think is the right thing to do:

He ought to change his job if he's not happy there.
It ought to be possible to buy a ticket in advance.

to give advice. *Ought to* is stronger than *should* in this use:

You ought to phone your mother, you know.
People ought not to drop their litter on the pavement.

to ask other people for advice or opinion:

Do you think we ought to ring the police?

Usage note

You can also use *ought to* + *have* + past participle to talk about past correct actions or obligations which someone did not do:

You ought to have waited until the lights turned green before you stepped into the road. That lorry might have knocked you down.
He oughtn't to have gone away without telling them.

Must

He must work harder or he'll fail.

You can use *must* to talk about what it is necessary to do and cannot be avoided. It is the strongest way that you can give advice or tell someone what to do. It is stronger than *should* and *ought to*.

You can use *must* to show that you think something is absolutely necessary or to order someone to do something:

He must work much harder or he'll never pass his exam.
Must I finish all this work this afternoon?
They must wear safety belts whilst the plane is taking off.

and you can use *must not* to talk about something which you think it is necessary not to do or to order someone not to do something:

We mustn't miss the last train; we'll never get home.
Visitors to the zoo must not feed the animals.

You can use *must* to talk about what you feel sure is true now or in the future:

It's very unusual for Tim not to come to work: he must be ill.
I'm hungry! It must be time for lunch.

NOTE **that you use the infinitive without *to*. This use sounds much more certain than *may* or *might*.**

In questions and negative sentences, you use can and can't:

It can't be time to go already: we've only been here an hour!
Who can that be? – It must be Donna.

You can use *must have* + past participle to make deductions about the past:

What was that noise? – It must have been thunder.
The Simons must have left. Their flat has been empty for days.

but in questions and negative sentences, you use *can have* and *can't have*:

They can't have told the milkman because he's left some milk.
Can he have forgotten, do you think? – He must have.

Dare

I daren't ask him for any more money.

You can use *dare* as a modal verb:

in questions and negative sentences. It means 'be brave enough to':

Dare we leave in the middle of the speech?
I daren't ask him for any more money.

and in the past tense:

They dared not step into the water: it was so rough it could have carried them away.
The dog growled at her again. She dared not move.

Usage note

You can use *How dare . . .!* to show that you are angry or annoyed:

How dare you shout at me in that rude way!
How dared he complain after all the trouble we'd taken!

You can also use *dare* as an ordinary verb:

You can use *do* + *dare* + infinitive to make negatives and questions:

He didn't dare to pick up the parcel in case it was a bomb.
Do you dare tell him you are looking for another job?
He wouldn't dare steal the jewellery.

NOTE that the infinitive is often used without *to*.

You can use *I dare you to* + infinitive to challenge someone to do something frightening. Children usually use this:

I dare you to try and get that bird's nest up there.
Why did you jump off the wall? – Johnnie dared me to.

Need

Need I come in to work tomorrow?

You can use *need* as a modal verb:

to ask questions, about the present or future. You are often asking permission, especially permission not to do something:

Need I come in to work tomorrow?
(Is it necessary to come into work tomorrow?)
Need he stay until the end? He has a long journey back.

and to make a negative when you are talking about an immediate necessity:

You needn't bother to finish that now.
We needn't phone and tell him: he'll be expecting us.
I don't think you need apply this year.

Usage note

You can use *needn't have* + past participle to talk about something you did in the past which was not necessary. In other words, you wasted your time doing it:

I needn't have hurried. No one else was there when I arrived.
You needn't have woken me up. My alarm was set to wake me.

You can also use *need* as an ordinary verb which is followed by the infinitive, to talk about the past, present and future:

She needs to get a new pair of spectacles. She can hardly see.
Do I need to take a lot of money with me?
How much food will we need to prepare?
We didn't need to explain anything. They understood.
You shouldn't need to wait long – the buses come quite frequently.

NOTE that this is a main verb, so you make questions and negatives with *do*, etc.

Used to

I used to smoke heavily but I gave it up three years ago.

You use *used to* to talk about the past:

about something which you did regularly in the past and which you do not do now:

I used to smoke heavily but I gave it up three years ago.
She used to go to work on her bike but she uses the car now.
They didn't use to drive a car in those days.

or about a past situation which no longer exists:

We used to live in South Road until we moved here.
Did you use to play football at school?
I really like vegetables now but I didn't use to when I was young.

Form

***Used to* has no present form. For present habits and situations you use the simple present tense.**

Positive
I used to work

Negative	**Short form**
I did not use to work	I didn't use to work
I used not to work	I usedn't to work (both formal)

Question
Did you use to work . . .?
Used you to work . . .? (formal)

Negatives

I **haven't** finished yet.

You can make a sentence, or the meaning of a sentence, negative in many different ways:

by using *not* with *be*, *do*, *have* or one of the modal verbs:

It isn't here.
My parents aren't coming after all.
We haven't managed to find the key.
Jane can't swim; she's still learning how to.

by using *not* with *do* in the present simple tense, and *did* in the past simple tense:

I don't like this dress: the colour doesn't suit me.
You didn't meet my brother last year, did you?

Or you can make a negative sentence by using a different negative word. You can use *never* or other adverbs with a negative meaning:

He has never been to see us since we moved.
They rarely go out after dark.

NOTE that you put *never*, etc. after the modal verb but before the main verb. Other words you can use like this are *rarely*, *seldom*, *hardly ever*, *scarcely*, *barely*.

You can use *no* + noun or *none* or *none of* + noun:

There was no food in the house and Mrs Jones had none to give us.
No dogs are allowed in the restaurant.
None of his friends have been able to help him.

These give emphasis to what you are saying, but are less usual than using *not* + verb + *a/any*:

We haven't any stamps left.
We have no stamps left.

You can use *no one*, *nobody*, *nothing*, or *nowhere*:

No one would give me a lift to the station.
I can find nothing wrong with you.

You can use *neither* + singular noun or *neither of* + plural noun:

Neither parent wants to leave the baby.
Neither of these films is suitable for a child.

You use *neither* when you are talking about two people or two things. It means not one and not the other.

You can use *neither* or *nor* to make negative agreements and replies in a conversation:

I don't like rice much. – Neither do I.
Joan can't drive. – Nor can Hilda.

Usage notes

You use only one negative word in a sentence.

After a negative, *some*, *something*, *somebody*, *somewhere* change to *any*, *anything*, *anybody*, *anywhere*, and *already* changes to *yet*.

I've already found somewhere to live.
I haven't found anywhere to live yet.

Form

The short forms of the negatives are as follows:

do not – don't, does not – doesn't
did not – didn't
has not – hasn't, have not – haven't
will not – won't
cannot – can't

Usage note

Use the short negative *n't* when you speak or when you write informally, for example, a note to a friend.

Use the full negative *not* when you write a formal letter or when you want to emphasise the negative when you are speaking.

Questions

Is it raining in York?

You make questions by:

changing the word order where *be*, *do*, *have* or a modal verb is used with a main verb:

I can see it. – Can you see it?
It's raining in York. – Is it raining where you are?
I've been waiting ages. Have you been waiting long?
They are Scottish. Are they from Edinburgh?

using *do* when there is only a main verb in the present simple tense:

I live in Chester Road. Do you live round here?
He works in Booths. Does his girlfriend work there?

and using *did* with a main verb in the past simple tense:

She passed her driving test. – Did he pass his?
We watched the film last night. Did you watch it?

using a question word like *who*, *what*, *where*, *why*, *when* and *how*:

The match will start at 3 o'clock. When will it finish?
I'm meeting Jane outside the station. Where shall I meet you?
Which one would Jane like? The strawberry one.
Freddie told me. Who told you?

NOTE: you must still change the word order.

What do you want for dinner?
Who did he hit?
Why didn't he ask me first?

NOTE: you use *do* or *did*.

using a question tag like *isn't it?* at the end of a sentence:

You speak French, don't you? Yes, I do.
He can drive, can't he? Yes, I think so.
I'll get in all right, won't I? I'm sure you will.
It's got very dear, hasn't it? Yes, it has.
They didn't get in touch, did they? No, they didn't.

Form

Statement	**Question**
with main verb only:	
You like coffee	Do you like coffee?
Jan works there	Does Jan work there?
We met him last year	Did we meet him last year?
with *be, do, have* or modal + main verb:	
I must leave	Must I leave?
You can phone him	Can you phone him?
He is arriving today	Is he arriving today?
It hasn't stopped yet	Hasn't it stopped yet?
with *be, do, have* + modal + main verb:	
(change the order of the subject and the first modal)	
It's been raining	Has it been raining?
They've been told	Have they been told?
I should have known	Should I have known?

with question words:

When can we start the course?
Where should I ask about it?
What do you like watching on TV?
Why didn't she ask someone?
How old is John?
Which one shall we have?

***who* asks about the subject of the sentence:**

Who likes Sally? Ann and Jane like her.

or about the object of the sentence:

Who does Sally like? She likes Jo and Bob.

***who* and *what* can both ask about the subject:**

Who told you about my new job?
Who can help us move the car?
What happened?
What made that funny noise?

The infinitive

He wants **to see** you now.

You can use the infinitive form of the verb, *to be*, *to make*, *to go*, etc. after some other verbs:

I don't want to get a new cassette recorder yet.
He hopes to have some new stock by Thursday.
We refused to give them any more information by phone.
Will you promise not to be so late again?
They ought to have known better than that!

There is a list of verbs which you can use with the infinitive at the end of this section (page 70).

You can use the infinitive after some verb + object phrases:

She has invited her mother to stay for a few days.
I asked them to talk more quietly.
He told his wife not to phone him at the office.
His supervisor allows him to go home early sometimes.
Who advised you to buy this make of car?

There is a list of verbs which you can use with an object + infinitive at the end of this section (page 70).

Usage note

Some verbs can be used in both of these ways, but with a difference in meaning:

I want to study electronics at university.
I want my daughter to study electronics at university.
We're expecting to arrive in Dublin at 5pm.
We're expecting my aunt to arrive in Dublin at 5pm.
He asked to speak to the manager.
He asked me to speak to the manager for him.

These verbs are *ask*, *expect*, *hate*, *help*, *intend*, *like*, *mean*, *prefer* and *want*.

You can use some verbs with the question words *how*, *what*, *when*, *where*, *which*, *who*, *whether* + *to* + infinitive:

I couldn't find out where to get my tyre repaired.
Do you know how to repair it yourself?
Can you remember what to do?
He hasn't decided whether to go to France or Italy.

The most common verbs in this group are *ask*, *decide*, *discover*, *find out*, *forget*, *know*, *learn*, *remember*, *understand*, *wonder* and *show/tell* + object.

You can use the infinitive after a verb to show why you do something:

They've come to watch the carnival.
He's gone to the bank to cash a cheque.
We're going to Cookham tomorrow to see our new house.
I stopped for twenty minutes to choose some books.
We needed an early start to get there in one day.
She started working in the evenings to earn some extra money.

This use is very common after *come* and *go* but you can use an infinitive to show purpose after any verb.

Usage note

A small group of verbs are followed by the infinitive without *to*. These are *let*, *make*, *feel*, *hear*, *see*, *watch* + object:

Don't let the children play outside in the cold for too long.
The government made the unions agree to a 5% pay increase.
Did you see a man get out of the car and go into that house?
We heard a car start up and drive off down the road.
I watched him walk down the street.

and the modal verbs *can*, *may*, *might*, *must*, *shall*, *should*, *will*, *would* and *could*:

We can go in the morning.
All applicants must return their forms by 21 April.
You will feel better in the morning.

The infinitive with nouns and pronouns

I've been given a lot of work to finish today.

You can use the infinitive after a noun or pronoun to show what you are going to do with it:

I've been given a lot of work to finish today.
Can I offer you something to eat?
Would you like a book to read on the train? – No, it's all right thanks. I've already got one to take.
She needs a black hat to wear to her uncle's funeral.

Sometimes you need a preposition after the infinitive:

My son gets lonely: he wants a friend to play with.
(A child plays with a friend.)
He has found a new flat to move into.
(You move into a new flat.)
You'll need a corkscrew to open that bottle with.
Can I get you a box to keep those things in?
There's a lot to talk about.

You use an infinitive in the phrase *for* + noun/pronoun + *to* + infinitive:

It will be easy for Dominic to pass his French exam: his mother's French and he speaks it well.
It's too late for us to go shopping now.
Are you looking for somewhere to sit down?
No, I'm waiting for my husband to come back.

The infinitive with adjectives

I was pleased **to see** him again!

You can use the infinitive after adjectives of mood and feelings like *happy* and *angry*:

I was so pleased to see him again after all this time!
We were surprised to hear that he's left for Japan.
She will be relieved to know that her child is safe.
They are very sad to have to leave.

Adjectives like this are *anxious*, *happy*, *sad*, *pleased*, *glad*, *angry*, *surprised*, *disappointed*, *ready* and *willing*.

You can use the infinitive after some adjectives and their comparative and superlative forms:

It's easy to see why she won the athletics trophy.
This fruit cake is easier to make than the sponge.
But this one would be the easiest to do.
It was impossible to get on the train.

Adjectives like this are *easy*, *difficult*, *good*, *interesting*, *boring*, *nice*, *possible*, *silly*, *stupid* and *wrong*.

You can use an infinitive after the phrase *it is/was* + adjective + of noun/pronoun:

It was silly of you to speak to a stranger!
(You were silly to speak to a stranger!)
It was good of Mrs Thomas to come and help us.
It's kind of you to offer.

You can use an infinitive after *too* + adjective and after an adjective + *enough*:

He says he's too tired to come out with us tonight.
Are you strong enough to carry all that luggage?
This drawer isn't big enough to keep files in.

Form

You can also use the infinitive in the negative, in the continuous form, in the past form and in the passive form:

You form the negative by putting *not* in front of the infinitive:

I decided not to go skiing again.
We asked you not to tell anyone.
You might not find the right road.

You form the continuous infinitive with *to be* + *-ing*:

He pretended to be working when he was really sleeping.
They may be waiting at the station for you.

You form the past infinitive with *to have* + *-ed* (past participle):

He seems to have lived in Italy most of his life.
We ought to have told them where we were.

You form the passive infinitive with *to be* + *-ed* (past participle):

I want to be told the whole truth.
This form has to be filled in and returned by 5 May.

These verbs can be followed by the infinitive:

agree, appear, arrange, ask, attempt, begin, beg, can afford, choose, consent, dare, decide, demand, determine, expect, fail, forget, happen, hate, help, hope, intend, learn, like, love, manage, mean, need, neglect, offer, plan, prefer, prepare, pretend, promise, propose, refuse, remember, seem, start, swear, threaten, try, not trouble, want, wish

These verbs can be followed by an object + infinitive:

advise, allow, ask, beg, bribe, cause, command, compel, direct, encourage, expect, forbid, force, get, hate, help, instruct, intend, invite, leave, like, mean, need, order, permit, persuade, prefer, recommend, remind, request, teach, tell, want, warn, urge

The -ing form

Smoking is not allowed in the restaurant.

You can use the *-ing* form of the verb (also called verbal noun or gerund):

as the subject or object in a sentence, especially when you are talking in general about something:

Smoking is not allowed in the restaurant.
John's favourite sport is swimming.
I know reading in the dark is bad for your eyes.

The *-ing* form can have its own object or adverb phrase:

Riding a bike is dangerous in heavy traffic.
Living in the country is so relaxing after the city.
Hearing her voice again made him very happy.

after a preposition:

She is fond of seeing her nieces and nephews.
I'm not keen on gardening.
They're only interested in listening to records.
He was fined for parking on a double yellow line.
We're looking forward to seeing you soon.
You get tired of working at night.

You can use the *-ing* form after some verbs:

I've started going to keep-fit classes.
We've finished painting the bathroom; it looks nice.
When did you stop smoking?
She hates getting up very early in the morning.
They deny knowing anything about it.

and after some phrasal verbs:

I keep on bumping into things; I must need glasses.
You must see about getting the car fixed.
We are against giving firearms to the police.
She has put off going to the dentist all year and now she needs three fillings.
He gave up drinking alcohol after his operation.

with the verb *do* to talk about a job of work:

I'm going to do some shopping on my way home tonight.
He has to do his studying at night.
They did all the decorating last weekend.

These verbs can be followed by the *-ing* form:

admit, anticipate, appreciate, avoid, consider, delay, deny, detest, dislike, dread, enjoy, escape, excuse, fancy, finish, forgive, hate, imagine, involve, keep, loathe, love, mind, miss, postpone, prevent, propose, remember, resent, resist, risk, save, start, stop, suggest, understand, prefer

You can also use the *-ing* form after these phrases:

It's no use/good/fun . . .
It's not worth . . .
I/he etc. can't stand . . .
I/he etc. can't help . . .

The infinitive or the -ing form?

He stopped **to buy** a paper./
He stopped **buying** a paper.

After some verbs you can use the infinitive or the *-ing* form. With some verbs there is no difference in meaning, but with others the meanings of the two forms are very different:

You use the infinitive or the *-ing* form after *hate*, *like*, *love* and *prefer* with no difference in meaning:

I love watching old films but I also like to see new ones sometimes.

We prefer eating early in the evening because we don't like going to bed right after a meal.

but you use *like* + infinitive to talk about something which you think you must do or choose to do but may not enjoy:

I like to go to the dentist's every six months and have my teeth checked.

I didn't like to ring you last night because it was so late, so I'm ringing now instead.

and you always use the infinitive after *would like*, *would prefer*, *would love* and *would hate*:

She'd love to visit her daughter in Australia.

We'd prefer to come on Thursday, if that's all right.

You can use either the infinitive or the *-ing* form after the verbs *begin*, *start*, *continue*, *intend* and *propose* with no difference in meaning:

He intends changing/to change his car this year.

We began clearing the flat at 10 and continued to work until James arrived.

After the verbs *forget*, *remember*, *go on*, *stop* and *regret* you use the *-ing* form to talk about something which you have done:

They will never forget meeting the Queen.
I remember being chased by a bull when I was a young child.
He has only stopped smoking recently.
She went on travelling the world until she was 80.

and you use an infinitive to talk about something which you decide you will do:

They forgot to reserve tickets and the theatre was full when they arrived.
You'll remember to pick up the bread when you go out, won't you?
He stopped the engine to light a cigarette.
She went on to write the story of her life at 85.

You use *try* with the *-ing* form when you talk about making an experiment or doing something to see what will happen:

I can't make this radio work. – Have you tried putting a new battery in it?
She tried cutting out all sweet food and she lost 5 kilos.

and *try* with an infinitive when you talk about making an effort or attempting to do something difficult:

I'm trying to make this radio work but I can't find anything wrong with it.
She tried to cut out all sweet food but it was too difficult.

After the verbs *see*, *hear* and *watch* you use the infinitive without *to* to talk about a complete action:

I heard a girl cry out in pain.
(She cried once and I heard the cry.)
We watched Simon swim across the lake.
(We saw the whole swim from one side to the other.)

and you use the *-ing* form to talk about part of an action:

I heard a girl crying out in pain.
(She was crying for some time but I only heard part of the crying.)
We watched Simon swimming across the lake.
(We saw part of the swim.)

Reported speech

He says he's leaving now.

When you want to report what someone says or thinks, you can either use their exact words (Direct Speech):

'I often spend my weekends in the flat,' John says.

or you can use a reporting verb and change their original words slightly without changing the meaning (Indirect or Reported Speech):

John says that he often spends his weekends in the flat.

The main reporting verbs are *say* and *tell*:

They say that they aren't going away this year.
She says she wants another cup of tea.
Chris tells me his job is very tiring.
I told Mrs Stacy last week that I couldn't help.

When you use *tell*, you must say who you tell:

Anna said that she wanted to leave.
Anna told me that she wanted to leave.

NOTE **that you don't have to use *that* with these verbs.**

Other reporting verbs are *agree*, *answer*, *admit*, *be sure*, *complain*, *explain*, *know*, *mention*, *promise*, *remark*, *reply*, *shout*, *suggest*, *think*, etc.:

We agreed that it was better to have another meeting.
He's fairly sure he'll be able to finish it by Friday.
The policeman explained that the prisoner had escaped very early that morning.
They know they haven't got enough time to go.
The professor admitted that he did not know the answer but (he) thought he could find it for me.

orting in the present tense

se the present tense when you report a conversation that is oing on (for example, on the telephone) or read out a letter or uctions. Do not change the tense of the words you report:

he says she is just leaving and will be here in half an hour.
 ('I'm just leaving. I'll be there in half an hour.')
promise I'll do all I can to help.
 ('I'll do all I can to help, I really will.')
They write that the weather is good and that they have been swimming every day.
 ('The weather's good. We've been swimming every day.')
It explains that the motor sometimes gets too hot.
 ('The motor sometimes gets too hot.')

and you use the present tense to report something which is always true or happens very often:

Jane says she'll never go abroad because she hates travelling.
He admits he is always forgetting things!

Reporting in the past tense

When you report what someone said in the past, the reporting verb is in the past tense and you usually change their words into a past tense:

He told me that he lived in Scotland.
 ('I live in Scotland.')
She explained she had lived in America in her teens.
 ('I lived in America in my teens, you see.')
The footballer complained that his ankle was hurting.
 ('Ah! My ankle's hurting!')
The man agreed that it had been a terrible year.
 ('Yes, it's been a terrible year.')

but when you report in the past something which is always true, you can use the past or present tense to report their words:

He told me that he lives in Scotland.
Maria said she liked cooking Italian food.
Maria said she likes cooking Italian food.
 ('I like cooking Italian food.')

Form

Direct speech or question	Reported speech or question
Present simple tense	**Past simple tense**
am/is	was
are	were
has/have	had
like/likes	liked
Present continuous tense	**Past continuous tense**
am/is living	was living
are living	were living
Present perfect simple tense	**Past perfect simple tense**
have/has lived	had lived
Past simple tense	**Past simple tense or Past perfect tense**
lived	lived or had lived
Past continuous tense	**Past continuous tense or Past perfect continuous tense**
was living	was living or had been living
Future	**Conditional tense**
will	would
must	had to

Usage notes

When you report what someone else has said, you must change any words which refer directly to that person:

Pronouns

I	–	he/she
we	–	they
this	–	it
these	–	they/them

Adjectives

my	–	his/her
our	–	their
this/that	–	the

and adverbs which refer to the original time and place:

now	–	then
here	–	there
today	–	that day
yesterday	–	the day before
tomorrow	–	the next day
next week	–	the following week
last year	–	the year before

Reporting questions

You use the reporting verbs *ask*, *enquire*, *want to know*, *wonde* report questions.

She wants to know if she can come at 10 o'clock instead of
He asked me if I had anything to declare.
We enquired where the tourist office was.
I wonder why the train is so late.

NOTE that you do not use question word order when you rep questions.

You do not use a question mark for reported questions.

You must change the tense of the question in the same way as you do when you report statements.

When you report questions, you use the reporting verb + *if* or *whether*:

She asked if she could leave early.
('Can I leave early?')
Someone wants to know if there's a train to Hurley this afternoon.
('Is there a train to Hurley this afternoon?')
We enquired if anyone in the hotel spoke French.
('Does anyone here speak French?')
I wondered whether the fish was fresh.
('Is the fish fresh?')

but when you report questions which use a question word, you use a reporting verb + a question word (*what*, *when*, *where*, *which*, *who*, *why*, *how*, etc.):

He asked me what I wanted.
('What do you want?')
They want to know when the coach leaves.
('When does the coach leave?')
We wondered why they hadn't phoned us.
('Why haven't they phoned us?')
The doctor called and enquired how I was feeling.
('Good morning, Mrs Smith. How are you feeling now?')

When you report orders and requests, you use *tell/ask* + object + infinitive (with *to*):

The police told the crowd to stay behind the barrier.
The headmaster has told you many times not to leave this door open.
She asked us to turn our music down.
I'm asking everyone again not to be late.

or you can use *must/have to* for an order:

My trainer says I must practise three hours a day.
The doctor told me I had to stop smoking.

You also report advice and recommendations, invitations, reminders and warnings with a reporting verb + object + infinitive (with *to*):

Our solicitor advised us not to take any action.
Did you invite your sister to come with us?
She reminded them to arrive early for the exam.
I warned them to be very careful on the ice.

and you report agreements, offers, promises, refusals and threats with a reporting verb + infinitive (with *to*):

The bank has agreed to lend us £1000.
My neighbour has offered to feed the cat while we're away.
He promised to finish the work by the end of the week.
His father has refused to lend him any more money.
We threatened to call the police if they did not go.

After some reporting verbs, you use the *-ing* form of the verb:

She accused him of stealing money from her purse.
He admitted taking the money.
They apologised for arriving so late.
The young man insisted on paying for all the drinks.
The man denies knowing anything about the stolen car.
My parents have suggested going out for a meal.

Phrasal Verbs

She **gave up** smoking last year.

Many English verbs are made up of two or three parts: a main verb and an adverb or a preposition:

The car broke down on the way to the airport.
As soon as I get up in the morning I turn on the radio.

These verbs, called phrasal verbs, do not mean the same as the main verbs alone:

break down means 'stop working'
get up means 'get out of bed'
turn on means 'make operate'

Phrasal verbs are either transitive or intransitive. Intransitive phrasal verbs do not have a direct object after them:

The plane takes off at eight o'clock tomorrow morning.
Sit down and shut up!

Transitive phrasal verbs must have a direct object after them:

We gave away a lot of furniture when we moved into our flat.
He put off his holiday because he was ill.
You must hand your homework in on Friday.

As these examples show, the direct object can usually come either before or after the adverb or preposition:

She made a story up for the children.
She made up a story for the children.
Look up the word in the dictionary.
He looked the word up in the dictionary.

When the direct object is a long phrase, you must put it after the adverb or preposition:

I had to turn down the chance to go to America because I was too busy at work.
He gave all the money back.
He gave back all of the money that he owed them.

When the direct object is a pronoun, you must put it before the adverb or preposition:

Put down that vase. Put it down before you drop it!
Is that Annie outside? Let her in, will you?
I gave up cigarettes this month. – Did you? I gave them up last year.
We'll pick you up at your house at eight o'clock. Okay?
Ring him up and ask him if he wants to come with us.

Some common phrasal verbs are listed below. We show the usual position of their direct objects. Use your dictionary to find out the meaning of them:

ask

ask for: He asked for another sandwich.

break

break down (no object): The car broke down on the way to work.
break into: They broke into the shop and stole all the cash.
break up: The police tried to break the meeting up.
They tried to break up the meeting.

bring

bring back: Some people want to bring hanging back for murder.
They want to bring back hanging.
bring up: She wants to bring crime up at the meeting.
She wants to bring up crime.

come

come from: Anna comes from Warsaw.
come out (no object)

do

do up: She's doing the cottage up at weekends.
She's doing up the cottage at weekends.
do with: I could do with a cup of tea now.
do without: I had to do without my tea. There was no milk.

get

get along (no object)
get at: I couldn't quite get at the shelf. It was too high.
get away (no object)

get away with: The thieves got away with one million pounds.
get back (no object)
get by (no object)
get in (no object)
get into: I can't get into these jeans. I must be getting fat.
get on (no object)
get on with: How are you getting on with your new manager?
get out of: I couldn't get out of cutting the grass.
get together (no object)
get up (no object)
get up to: John's getting up to something. He's too quiet!

give

give away: She gave her bike away when she moved.
She gave away her bike.
give back: She gave the book back when she'd finished it.
She gave back the book.
give in (no object)
give out: John gave the exam papers out to the students.
He gave out the exam papers.
give up: I gave up smoking last year.

go

go after: She went after that job in the bank.
go against: She went against her parents and joined the army.
go ahead (no object)
go back (no object)
go by (no object)
go for: I'll go for the paper.
go off (no object)
go on (no object)
go out (no object)
go over: She went over the work to check for mistakes.
go round (no object)

let

let down: He let John down when he needed help.
He let down John when he needed help.
let in: You can let the guests in now.
You can let in the guests now.
let off: The police let John off with just a warning.
They let off John with a warning.

look

look after: Will you look after the dog for me, please?
look for: I'm looking for my glasses. Have you seen them?
look forward to: We're looking forward to the party.
look up: Look the word up in a dictionary.
Look up the meaning of the word in a dictionary.

make

make out: She made the cheque out to the shop.
She made out the cheque.
make up: He made the story up.
He made up the story.

put

put off: She put the meeting off until Friday.
She put off the meeting.
put on: Put your coat on. It's cold outside.
Put on your coat.
put out: Will you put the light out before you go to bed?
Will you put out the light?
put up: They keep putting their prices up.
They keep putting up their prices.
put up with: I will not put up with your rudeness any longer.

run

run away (no object)
run down: The bus ran the old man down.
The bus ran down the old man.
run into: I ran into Anna at the meeting.
run out of: We've run out of bread again!
run over: The bus ran the old man over.
The bus ran over the old man.

take

take after: He takes after his father.
take down: I took their address down.
I took down their address.
take off: He took his coat off and sat down.
He took off his coat and sat down.
take over: Anna took the business over last year.
Anna took over the business last year.
take up: She took water-skiing up this summer.
She took up water-skiing this summer.

Definite Article

The man has gone to **the** shops.

You use the definite article with singular and plural nouns:

when you talk about something which other people already know about:

Where's Mum? – She's just gone to the shops.
They're in the kitchen.
Shut the door, will you? It's cold.
I'm going to the park in a minute. Do you want to come?
Pass me the scissors, please. I need to cut this off.

or which you have already talked about before:

Mr Johnson has bought a new car; it's the blue Sierra over there.
There's a little boy and a girl in the playground: look, the girl's giving him a ride on a swing.

when you give some extra information about something so that we know exactly what you mean:

I still remember the day I went to London.
We'd like the seats next to the aisle.
Can you see the boy in the red jacket?

when there is only one example of something:

The weather was marvellous; the sun shone all day.
We flew over the Himalayas and had a boat trip down the Yangtse River.
I thought the Taj Mahal was wonderful.

when you use words like *biggest*, *best*, or *first*, *second*, *third*, or *only*, etc.:

The longest river in Europe is the Rhine.
The first time we met him was in 1982.
The most embarrassing situation I can remember is when I got on a train without any money.

Form

The form of the definite article never changes. It can be used with any singular or plural noun:

the house next to the station
the time I lost my handbag
the towns in the south of the country
the stars in the sky
the ones I like best
the people at the bus stop
the information on the timetable

Usage notes

You can also use the definite article with:

plural names of a whole family:

The Khans are having a party on Saturday.
Did you know the Smiths are moving to Bristol?

the names of some countries:

the USSR
the United Kingdom
the West Indies
the Netherlands

the names of rivers, canals and seas:

the Atlantic Ocean
the Mediterranean
the River Nile
the Thames

the names of theatres, cinemas, museums and hotels:

the Royal Academy
the Louvre
the Odeon, Leicester Square
the Great Western Hotel

and in some phrases with *of*:

the Houses of Parliament
the University of California

Indefinite Articles

I'd like **an** apple and **a** banana.

You use the indefinite article only with singular nouns:

when you talk about something for the first time:

I work in a hotel.
They live in an old house.
He has a bad headache.
There's a man outside who wants to speak to you.
My sister has just had a baby.

when you talk about something, and it isn't important which particular one you mean:

Can I have a glass of water, please?
Pass me a cloth, will you? I've spilt some coffee.
I'm going for a walk; see you in a minute.

when you describe someone or something:

I'm a farmer. Both my brothers are farmers too.
She's a good friend of mine.
He became an actor after he left the army.
It's a very hot day.

when you talk about price, speed and quantity:

The eggs are £1.20 a dozen; the cheese is £1.80 a kilo.
This silk costs £6 a metre.
The speed limit here is forty miles an hour.
She must take her medicine three times a day.
A lot of people came to listen to him; there were at least a hundred people there.

and in some exclamations:

What a pity! I really wanted to see that match.
What a lovely day!

Form

You use *a* before a word which begins with a consonant sound:

a man, a woman, a young child
a pint of milk
a European
a hundred pounds

NOTE that *European* begins with a vowel letter, but with a consonant sound, like *yes*.

You use *an* before a word which begins with a vowel sound:

an egg
an apple
an unhappy story
an idea
thirty miles an hour

NOTE that *hour* begins with a consonant letter, but with a vowel sound, like *our*.

Usage notes

The indefinite article is never used with plural nouns. Instead you can use words like *some* and *any*:

I can see two men. I can see some men. I can't see any men.

Some very common nouns can be used without any article at all: *home*, *work*, *bed*, *school*, *college*, *hospital*, *church*, *market*, *court*, *prison*, *sea*; *breakfast*, *lunch*, *dinner*, *tea*; *car*, *bus*, *train*, *bicycle*, etc.:

I left work early and got to college by six.
She's been in hospital for three weeks but she's coming home tomorrow.

but only when we talk about it for its main purpose:

He went to prison for two years for robbing a bank.
She went to the prison to visit her husband.
They go to work by bicycle, by car, or by train.
I always go home for lunch.
We have dinner at eight o'clock.

Nouns

The woman was driving a car.

Nouns are either countable or uncountable:

Countable nouns are seen as separate units and can be counted:

a car	two cars	twenty cars
one man	ten men	a hundred men
each cup	three cups	ten cups

they have singular and plural forms and you use them with singular and plural verbs:

A problem has cropped up which I'd like to discuss.
Some problems have come up which we must sort out.
The train is late this morning.
The trains are all late this morning because of the bad weather.

You can use *a/an* and numbers in front of them:

Would you like an apple?
You need four large apples to make this pie.
I just saw a child climb over that wall.
Three more children climbed over after him.

NOTE that you must always use singular countable nouns with a word like *a/an*, *the*, *this/that*, *my/your/his/hers/its*, etc.

You can use *many*, *not many*, *a lot of* and *a few* in front of them:

He doesn't have many friends.
I've got a few dresses here you might like.
A few spectators stayed until the end.
Are there many students coming to the party tonight?
There aren't many people here.
There are a lot of customers waiting to come in.

NOTE that you use *many* in questions and negative phrases and *a lot of* in positive phrases.

Uncountable nouns are not seen as separate units, and you cannot count them:

water	rain	sunshine	weather
tea	flour	bread	meat
advice	music	money	information
love	beauty	happiness	jealousy
earth	plastic	leather	furniture
dancing	smoking	parking	shopping

They have only one form and you always use them with a singular verb:

The rain has been very heavy this month.
There's more milk in the fridge if you need it.
All the land around here belongs to one farm.
My new furniture is arriving tomorrow.

You never use *a/an* or numbers in front of them:

I have some information for you.
The advice she was given was very confusing.
Is there any more bread? Yes, there's some here.
Have you had any news from the hospital yet?

You can use *much*, *not much*, *a little* and *a lot of* in front of them:

We don't have much time.
There isn't much petrol left in the car.
I'd like a little more information about the hotel.
Can you give him a little help with his homework?
Have you got much luggage to take on holiday?
There was a lot of rubbish lying around.

NOTE that you use *much* in questions and negative phrases and *a lot of* in positive phrases.

Usage note

You can use uncountable nouns in a countable way by using words like *piece*, *bit*, etc. + *of*:

a bottle of milk	two spoons of sugar
a glass of water	a few slices of bread
a sheet of paper	three pieces of furniture
a bit of chocolate	half a pint of beer
a bit of difficulty	two litres of oil

Special singular and plural nouns

The army is/are fighting in the south of the country.

Group (or collective) nouns refer to a particular group of people or things:

a group of houses — a pack of cards
a class of students — an army

You use the singular when you are thinking of the group as a whole:

The O'Riley family has lived in this town for years.
The army is fighting in the south of the country.

You can use the plural form when you are thinking of the group as individual members or people:

All the class are taking part in the school play.
The England team aren't playing well at the moment.

Some nouns are always plural. They always take a plural verb: *cattle*, *clothes*, *contents*, *earnings*, *goods*, *people*, *police*, *premises*, *quarters*, *riches*, *savings*, *troops*, *wages*:

The police are searching for two dangerous criminals.
The cattle are grazing in the fields.
These clothes are soaking! Take them off and get dry.

Pair nouns like *shorts* are always plural, even though you may be talking about only one item or thing. These include: *trousers*, *pyjamas*, *jeans*, *pants*, *spectacles*, *glasses*, *binoculars*, *scissors*, *pliers*, *shears*, *scales*:

My glasses aren't strong enough. I can't see properly.
These jeans are too tight. I need some larger ones.

but you can put *a pair of* in front of a pair noun to make it singular or to count it:

This pair of shorts should fit you.
I'm going to buy two new pairs of trousers to take on holiday.

Form

Regular nouns

You make the plural of a regular noun by adding *-s* or *-es* to the singular noun:

day – days, button – buttons, price – prices

You add *-es* to a noun ending in *-s, -ss, -sh, -z, -x, -ch, -tch*:

bus – buses, buzz – buzzes, fox – foxes, boss – bosses, wish – wishes, church – churches, patch – patches

Irregular nouns

You add *-es* to nouns ending in *-o*:

tomato – tomatoes, potato – potatoes

but note:

radio – radios, photo – photos, piano – pianos

You change nouns ending in a consonant + *-y* to consonant + *-ies*:

party – parties, factory – factories, baby – babies, story – stories

but you add *-s* to a noun ending in vowel + *-y*:

boy – boys, donkey – donkeys, storey – storeys

***calf, half, knife, leaf, life, loaf, self, sheaf, shelf, thief, wife, wolf* change *-f* or *-fe* to *-ves* in the plural:**

life – lives, knife – knives, shelf – shelves, leaf – leaves

and *scarf, hoof, wharf* take *-s* or *-ves* in the plural:

scarfs or scarves, hoofs or hooves

but all other nouns ending in *-f* or *-fe* have regular plurals:

roof – roofs, handkerchief – handkerchiefs

Some more irregular nouns are:

man – men, milkman – milkmen, woman – women, postwoman – postwomen, child – children, ox – oxen, mouse – mice, goose – geese, louse – lice, tooth – teeth, foot – feet

The possessive form

My **father's** car.

You use the possessive form of a noun:

to show that something belongs to someone:
This is my father's car.
Use John's pen – I'm sure he won't mind.

or that something is used by someone or a special group of people:
You'll find the ladies' toilet down there on the left.
The boys' school is on the other side of town.

You always use this form when you talk about people and animals:
You tie this leather strap round the horse's neck.
It was the children's choice to come here.
Shakespeare's plays have been performed here for years.
The government's policy has changed in the last year.

and you usually use it when you talk about place names and ships, boats, planes and other vehicles:
York's oldest buildings are around the cathedral.
The ship's cabins have recently been modernised.
Italy's exports have fallen this year.

in some phrases of time:
I've still got a week's/two weeks' holiday left this year.
Have you seen today's paper yet?
You get fifteen minutes' break between the films.

and in a shortened form when you mention a shop or a person's home:
I went to the butcher's but he didn't have any lamb.
(the butcher's shop)
Marks and Spencer's have some nice sweaters.
Chris has gone round to Anna's for the afternoon.
(Anna's house/home)

Form

To make the possessive form:

You add *-'s* to a singular noun and to plural nouns which do not end in *-s*:

a man's coat	the men's toilet
a woman's voice	women's dancing classes
that child's bike	a children's party
John's ticket	the people's choice

You can add *'s* to nouns which are made up of more than one word, and to initials or abbreviations:

my son-in-law's idea
the Duke of York's award
the USA's foreign policy (United States of America's)
the PM's question time (Prime Minister's)

You add the apostrophe (') after the *-s* to plural nouns which already end in *-s*:

a boys' cricket match
the girls' swimming lessons
two weeks' holiday
the passengers' information desk
five minutes' wait

when someone's name ends in *-s*, you can add *-'s* or the apostrophe only:

Frances's letter or Frances' letter
Mr Jones's car or Mr Jones' car

Personal Pronouns

He let **me** go with **them.**

You use a pronoun to talk about yourself or other people, and when we already know who or what you are talking about:

You use a subject pronoun (*I*, *you*, *he*, *she*, *it*, *we*, *you*, *they*) as the subject of a verb:

I recognise that man. He's Ali's brother.
You go ahead and catch the bus. It might be early.
We don't know when they'll be back.

Usage notes – *they*

You use *they* to talk about more than one person:

My daughters are 12 and 14 now. They both go to Trinity School.

You can also use *they* to talk about a group of people with some authority, like the government or the town council, or a group of people, especially when you do not know exactly who they are:

They are going to widen this road and build a pedestrian crossing.
They say this area used to be very pretty years ago.
They want to close the hospital but we mustn't let them!

Usage notes – *you*

You can use *you* to talk about people in general, including yourself:

You can get to Edinburgh in less than five hours on the new express.

You can also use *one* in this meaning. This is more formal:

One never knows if those adverts are truthful or not.

Usage notes – *it*

You can use *it* to talk about a thing or an animal (a bus, a bag, an elephant, a sparrow) but you can also use *it* to talk about a person when you ask or explain who the person is:

Who was that on the phone? – It was Jean.
Who is it? – It's me, Harry, open the door!

You use *it* to talk about the time, the weather and distances:

It's half past four and it's already getting dark.
It is very cold for the time of year.
How far is it to Liverpool? It must be at least 200 kilometres.

You often use *it* as the subject before the verbs *be*, *seem*, *appear*, *happen*, *look*, *depend*:

What is it? – It's difficult to say. It looks like soot. It seems odd. It looks as if he will be in hospital for another week at least. It depends on his head injury.

You can use *it* to replace the subject of the verb in a sentence when the subject is very long. The subject comes later in the sentence:

It's marvellous to see you again.
It must be difficult to live here without electricity.
It doesn't matter where you buy the materials.

You can sometimes use *it* to begin a sentence to give special emphasis to something you are talking about:

It was only last Wednesday that George and Ann left.
(instead of: George and Ann left last Wednesday.)
I bet it was Douglas who left the bikes outside.
(instead of: I bet Douglas left the bikes outside.)

You use an object pronoun (*me*, *you*, *him*, *her*, *it*, *us*, *you*, *them*) as the direct object of a verb:

Her teacher wants her to study science at university.
My cousin has invited us to his place on Sunday.

or as the indirect object of a verb:

The President gave him a medal for bravery.
Did John tell you the answer?

or after a preposition:

Can Jane look after it for me this afternoon?
He won't lend his car to them any more.

Form

Personal pronouns

Subject	**Object**	**Possessive**	**Reflexive**
Singular			
I	me	mine	myself
you	you	yours	yourself
he	him	his	himself
she	her	hers	herself
it	it	its	itself
Plural			
we	us	ours	ourselves
you	you	yours	yourselves
they	them	theirs	themselves

Possessive Pronouns

I like your suit. It fits better than **mine.**

You use a possessive pronoun (*mine*, *yours*, *his*, *hers*, *its*, *ours*, *yours*, *theirs*) to show that something belongs to someone:

I like your suit. It fits better than mine.
(mine = my suit)
Yours is a nicer colour, though.
(yours = your suit)
Where did Jane buy hers?
(hers = her suit)
We usually get ours in Marks & Spencer.
(ours = our suits)
Theirs are very good quality, aren't they?
(theirs = their suits)

Reflexive Pronouns

Frank has hurt himself.

You use a reflexive pronoun (*myself*, *yourself*, *himself*, *herself*, *itself*, *ourselves*, *yourselves*, *themselves*) to talk about the same person or thing as the subject:

I told myself not to be so silly.
Frank has hurt himself. Come and help me lift him up.
Have you ever asked yourself why you are so afraid of spiders?
Please help yourselves to some more food!
They could make themselves ill if they continue to live like that!

and when you want to emphasise that one person, and no other, does something:

And did you build the whole house yourself?
Yes, we had to do it ourselves because we didn't have enough money to pay a builder.

You also use it in some special phrases:

Does she live by herself? – No, her sister lives with her.
(by herself = on her own/alone)
The timer switches on by itself. You don't need to touch it.
(by itself = on its own/without any help)
Enjoy yourself at the dance tonight!
Make sure those children behave themselves and don't make too much noise.

Usage note

***themselves* and *each other* have different meanings:**

The boys looked at themselves in the mirror.
(each boy looked at his own face)
Peter and Tony looked at each other and smiled.
(Peter looked at Tony and Tony looked at Peter)

Demonstrative Pronouns

This tastes delicious!

You use the demonstrative pronouns (*this*, *that*, *these*, *those*) when we already know what you are talking about:

You use *this* to talk about a thing or a situation which is very near or which you are involved with or which is happening now:

This tastes delicious – did you make it yourself?
(this = food/cake/pie . . .)
This sounds dreadful. I think I'll turn it off.
(this = this music/record/concert . . .)
This is the kind of thing I've been looking for. You see? Here!

***these* is the plural of *this* so you use it to refer to several things which are here:**

These will do fine. Can I have a kilo of them, please?
(these = these apples/potatoes . . .)
These are the trousers I was telling you about. Do you like them or do you prefer those over there?

You use *that* to talk about something which is further away and which you are not involved with. It may be something which has finished:

That was really good. I haven't enjoyed myself so much for ages!
(that = that film/dance/party . . .)
Where did that come from? It looks very old.
That sounds like the dustmen coming along now.

***those* is the plural of *that* so you use it to refer to several things which are further away:**

I don't like these roses so much. I prefer those at the other end of the garden.
Would you like to try one of these hats? They're much cheaper than those over there.

Relative Pronouns

Is that the man **who** lives at No. 36?

The relative pronouns (*who*, *whom*, *whose*, *which*, *that*) introduce more information about someone or something. They join together two clauses in a sentence:

You use *who* or *that* to explain which person you are talking about. *Who* is more usual:

The woman who works in the corner shop has won the lottery.
(A woman has won the lottery. She works in the corner shop.)
We want to speak to the shop assistant who served us yesterday.
(A shop assistant served us yesterday. We want to speak to him.)
The person that told me about the boat has been on it himself.
(A person told me about the boat trip. The person has been on it himself.)
I hate people that shout.
(Some people shout. I hate those people.)

You use *which* and *that* to explain which thing, idea or animal you mean:

The school needs a bus which can carry 10 passengers.
The book that won the Booker prize this year was made into a film.
The thing that really annoyed me was the long wait.

***who*, *which*, *that* can be left out of the clause when the two verbs have different subjects:**

The soup (which/that) you made was delicious.
That old man (who/that) you were laughing at is my grandfather.

You use *whose* to explain who someone or something belongs to:

I know someone whose brother is in the rugby club.
This is Anika whose class you will be in.

Usage notes

You can use *whom* instead of *who* to explain which person you mean when the person is the object of the verb. This use is formal:

The couple whom I met on holiday live in the next street.
(The couple live in the next street. I met the couple on holiday.)

but it is more usual to use *who* or leave out *who* or *whom* altogether:

I can't see the man (who) I gave the documents to.
There isn't anyone (who) she can turn to for help.

Sometimes the verb in the relative clause has a preposition after it. You can move the preposition in front of *which*, *whom*, *whose*, but this is formal:

The chair collapsed. Fred was sitting on the chair.
The chair (that/which) Fred was sitting on collapsed.
The chair on which Fred was sitting collapsed.
The man over there is the principal. John was talking to the man just now.
The man over there (who/that) John was talking to just now is the principal.
The man to whom John was talking is the principal.

You can use *why*, *when*, *where* like relative pronouns to give more information about a reason, a time or a place. You can leave these out too:

Do you know the reason (why) he won't come?
I can still remember the day (when) we first met.
Did you like that place where we had our picnic?
Did you like that place we had our picnic at?

Adjectives

I need two strong plastic bags.

An adjective gives you information about a noun. It tells you what something is (*a blue car*) or what it seems like (*he looks ill*).

An adjective never changes its form. It stays the same with singular, plural, masculine or feminine nouns:

An old man was sitting on the bench.
Two old men walked up and sat down next to him.
I could see an old woman feeding the birds.

An adjective is placed in front of the noun it describes:

That was a beautiful song.
I've got a new winter coat.
Several scruffy little boys ran past.

or on its own after the verbs *be*, *appear*, *feel*, *look*, *seem*, *smell*, *sound*, *taste*:

That song was beautiful.
This coat's new. It looks smart, doesn't it?
He feels sick. He's not coming with us today.
I don't know her very well but she seems friendly.
This soup tastes wonderful. It smells good too.
It sounds very suspicious to me.

Some adjectives can only come after a verb and not in front of the noun which they describe. These are *afraid*, *alive*, *alone*, *asleep*, *awake*, *content*, *ill*, *well*:

I was afraid to tell them what had happened.
After two years' absence, he returned alive and well.

When you are giving measurements, the adjective comes after the measurement noun:

The garden is 25 metres long and about 5 metres wide.
The Pyramids are over 300 feet high.

Usage notes

When you have several adjectives in front of one noun:

next to the noun, you put an adjective which tells you what the noun is for – its purpose:

He's just bought a garden chair. (a chair for the garden)

in front of this, you put any adjective which tells you what something is made of:

He's bought a plastic garden chair.

before this, you put any adjective which tells you where something comes from – its origin:

He's bought an Italian plastic garden chair.

before this, you put colour adjectives:

He's bought a white Italian plastic garden chair.

in front of these, you put adjectives of quantity, size, shape, age, temperature and so on:

He's bought a new white Italian plastic garden chair.

NOTE that you only use *and* to join two colour adjectives or the last adjective to the others when they come after the verb:

I like that purple and red rug over there.
He looked cold, shaken and nervous when I found him.

You can make the meaning of an adjective much stronger by using an adverb like *very*, *really*, *too*, *terribly*, *extremely*, *completely* in front of it:

Chris is really good at tennis.
He was terribly tired when he got back from Scotland.
That was a very interesting lecture.

or you can use the adverbs *fairly*, *quite*, *rather*, *pretty* to make the adjective just a little stronger. *Fairly* is the weakest adverb to use and *rather/pretty* are the strongest:

Your English is quite good but it still needs more improvement.
I thought the film was rather slow.
It's a fairly long journey but it won't take more than four hours.

Comparison of Adjectives

My brother is **taller** than me.

You often need to compare something with one or more other things using an adjective. You want to say how it is similar to or different from the others. You use the comparative and superlative forms of the adjective to do this.

You make the comparative form:

by adding *-er* to an adjective if it is short:

Have you got any bigger boxes?
She needs something which is softer.
I would like to be thinner.
I think the pink cover is prettier.

or by putting *more* in front of the adjective if it is long:

This wine is more expensive but it's very mellow.
This is a more direct route out of town.

You make the superlative form:

by putting *the* in front of the adjective and adding *-est* to the end of it, if it is short:

Toby is the tallest boy in the class.
That was the shortest tennis match I've ever seen.
Which is the loveliest spot along the coast?
We visited the highest lake in the world while we were in Peru.

or by putting *the most* in front of the adjective if it is long:

The most popular bar around here has always been Carla's.
We can leave the most difficult part to the end.
He must be the most famous person I've ever met.
What is the most frightening experience you've ever had?

NOTE **that short adjectives are *big*, *small*, *soft*, *cheap*, *tall*, *short*, *long*, *dark*, *thin*, *fat*, *clever*, *high*, *ugly*, *pretty*, *lovely*, etc.**

Long adjectives include most which are two syllables and all which are three syllables or more, e.g. *expensive*, *helpful*, *certain*, *famous*, *popular*, etc.

Usage notes

You can use *than* with the comparative form to complete the comparison:

My boots are very warm. Would you like to borrow them?
They would be warmer than your shoes.
Delo's is a very cheap place to buy clothes.
It's cheaper than all the other stores.
I thought his latest film was more entertaining than his previous ones.
This suitcase is more suitable for us than the others.

You can make your comparative adjective stronger by putting an adverb like *much*, *far*, *a lot*, *a little*, *a bit* in front of it:

The Fiat is much faster than the bigger cars.
Brighton is a bit further than Hove but it's a lot more interesting.

You can also compare things using *not as* + adjective *as* . . .:

Bertie's is not as cheap as Delo's.
Your shoes can't be as warm as my boots.
His earlier films weren't as entertaining as this one.
I'm not as quick at volleyball as I used to be.

and you can use the positive form of *as . . . as* to show that two things are the same:

The Fiat is just as expensive as the Renault.
It's as economical on petrol as the other car.
Is he still as keen on football as he was at school?
Marilyn Monroe is as popular now as she was 20 years ago.

You use the superlative form when you want to compare something or someone with all the others of its kind. You often use phrases like *in the world*, *in the family*, *I've ever known/seen/been to/had/met*, etc., to show you mean only one out of all possible ones.

Form

	Adjective	Comparative	Superlative
Short adjectives			
one syllable	short	shorter	the shortest
	new	newer	the newest
two syllables	easy	easier	the easiest
(ending in *-y*,	clever	cleverer	the cleverest
***-er*, *-e* or *-ly*)**	simple	simpler	the simplest
	lonely	lonelier	the loneliest
Long adjectives			
two syllables	helpful	more helpful	the most helpful
	famous	more famous	the most famous
three or more	difficult	more difficult	the most difficult
syllables	exciting	more exciting	the most exciting

Spelling notes

You change the *y* to *-ier* when you make the comparative form of adjectives ending in *-y*:

pretty – prettier, early – earlier, silly – sillier

You double the last consonant when you make the comparative form of short adjectives ending in a single consonant:

fat – fatter, thin – thinner, big – bigger

Some adjectives of two syllables can form the comparative and superlative in both ways: *clever*, *common*, *cruel*, *handsome*, *hollow*, *quiet*, *pleasant*, *shallow*, *simple*, *stupid*, *tired*, *wicked*:

pleasant	pleasanter	the pleasantest
	more pleasant	the most pleasant
wicked	wickeder	the wickedest
	more wicked	the most wicked

There are some irregular comparative and superlative forms:

Adjective	Comparative	Superlative
good	better	the best
bad	worse	the worst
little	less	the least
many/much	more	the most
far	further	the furthest

Adverbs

He walked **slowly** up the road.

An adverb gives you more information about a verb. Sometimes it gives you information about an adjective, another adverb or a whole sentence. An adverb can be either a single word (*quickly*) or a phrase (*in the morning*).

An adverb can tell you:

how something happens (an adverb of manner):
He walked slowly up to the seat and sat down carefully.
They can both speak Japanese fluently.

how often something happens (an adverb of frequency):
He always goes to see his grandmother on Sunday.
Have you ever been abroad?

Other adverbs of frequency are *usually*, *often*, *regularly*, *sometimes*, *occasionally*, *seldom*, *never*, *once*, *every week*, *twice a month*, *daily*, *from time to time*, etc.

when something happens (an adverb of time):
We're leaving tomorrow.
He hasn't come back yet. We are still waiting for him.

Other adverbs of time are *today*, *yesterday*, *now*, *soon*, *already*, *just*, *still*, *yet*, *on Sunday*, *last week*, *on Tuesday morning*, *in the end*, *eventually*, *afterwards*, etc.

where something happens (an adverb of place):
Can you wait outside, please?
He was sitting over there in the corner.

Other adverbs of place are *here*, *somewhere*, *at home*, *in the office*, *over there*, *downstairs*, *outside*, etc.

Other adverbs make the meaning of a verb, adjective or adverb stronger or weaker (an adverb of degree).

These adverbs can change the strength of an adjective:

He's an extremely noisy child.
The Majestic Hotel is too expensive now. I can't afford to stay there any more.
I'm not tall enough to join the army.

or another adverb:

They work very quickly at Stamford's.
He can walk fairly easily since his operation.

Use *very*, *too*, *completely*, *really*, *terribly*, *rather*, *fairly*, *quite*, *enough*, *so* with adjectives and adverbs.

or a verb:

I quite like opera but I don't know much about it.
We almost decided to buy a house but we weren't sure.
They really missed their mother when she was in hospital.
She can only come in the morning.

Use *almost*, *nearly*, *quite*, *rather*, *just*, *really*, *totally*, *completely*, *hardly*, *only*, *a lot*, *a little*, *a bit* with verbs.

or a comparative:

I feel much better after my rest.
You should find this a bit easier to read.
Does he drive any more carefully since his accident?

Use *much*, *a lot*, *a bit*, *a little*, *no*, *any*, *even* with comparatives.

Some adverbs tell you something about a whole sentence (sentence adverbs):

Actually, I'm not a teacher at all. I'm a technician.
Fortunately, they all recovered from the attack.
It will probably be all right.

Use *actually*, *fortunately*, *luckily*, *in fact*, *maybe*, *probably*, *perhaps*, *surely*, *certainly*, *obviously*, etc. as sentence adverbs.

Form

You make the comparative and superlative forms of adverbs in the same way as for adjectives:

you use adverbs ending in *-ly* with *more* + the adverb to form the comparative. You can use *than* to complete the comparison:

You must do your maths homework more accurately!
Could you repeat that more slowly, please?
She speaks Spanish more fluently than English.

you use adverbs ending in *-ly* with *the most* + the adverb to form the superlative:

Peter sings the most beautifully of all the choir.
Their father will talk about it the most readily.

you use adverbs with the same form as adjectives by adding *-er* to the adverb to form the comparative. You can use *than* to complete the comparison:

I get up earlier in the summer.
He sank deeper into the straw hoping no one would see.
It was later than I had realised.

you use adverbs with the same form as adjectives by adding *the* + *-est* to the adverb to form the superlative:

David could run the fastest of all his friends.
But Matthew ran the furthest.

Adverbs like this are *early*, *late*, *fast*, *hard*, *high*, *low*, *deep*, *far*, *straight*.

or you can make comparisons using *not as* + adverb *as*:

Fred can't play as well as his brother.
I don't go running as regularly as I used to.

adverbs with irregular comparative and superlative forms are:

well – better – the best, badly – worse – the worst, little – less – the least, much – more – the most, far – further – the furthest:

He plays the piano even worse than I do!

Usage notes

You can use adverbs in three different positions in a sentence:

in the front position, at the beginning of a sentence:
Surely you can't mean that!
Perhaps we could all go to the park this afternoon.

in the mid position:
I often do my housework before everyone gets up.
We can always ring you.

in the end position:
They rushed frantically towards the gates.
She can play the guitar very well.

Front position adverbs include:

sentence adverbs, which describe the whole sentence:
Surely you can't mean that!
Fortunately, we managed to get back before it started.
Perhaps we could all go to the park this afternoon.

adverbs and adverbial phrases of place and time:
In the shopping centre they play music all day long.
Afterwards he apologised for the trouble he'd caused.

adverbs of frequency (but not *always* or *never*):
Sometimes I don't get home until 10 o'clock.
Every week he takes fresh flowers to the cemetery.

the front position gives special emphasis to an adverb or adverbial phrase, so adverbs of manner sometimes come here:
Cautiously he turned the key and opened the door.
With a friendly wave he disappeared.

Mid position is either before the verb in the simple present/past tense or after *be*, *do* or *have*, or a modal verb. These include:

adverbs of frequency:
I often do my housework before everyone gets up.
They have seldom managed to complete the whole course.
He's never on time for class these days!

NOTE that longer adverbial phrases or *daily*, *every day*, *once a month*, etc. are used in end position.

adverbs of degree which are describing a verb:

We don't really mind if we can't go.
I rather like this colour, don't you?
Is the painting almost finished now?
They can only come on Monday.

NOTE that *much*, *a lot*, *a little*, *a bit* are used in end position.

a few adverbs of time like *just* and *still*, and the sentence adverbs *probably*, *certainly* and *definitely*:

He is just getting dressed. He won't be long.
I'm still waiting for someone to serve me!
It is certainly very cold for the time of year.

adverbs of manner are sometimes put in mid position, especially to describe people's actions:

He foolishly left his briefcase on the seat.
Would you kindly close the door after you?

End position is after the verb or the verb + the direct object. You never separate the verb and its object but you can put the adverb before or after prepositional phrases (for example *towards the gates*).

this is the most usual place for adverbs of manner:

They rushed frantically towards the gates.
He knows all Shakespeare's plays thoroughly.
She can play the guitar very well.

this is also the usual place for adverbs of time and place and certain adverbs of frequency like *every day*, *daily*, *weekly*, *on Sundays*, *twice a month*, etc.:

I'm sure he'll pass his driving test eventually.
He said he would let us know on Thursday.
They are watching television upstairs.

the adverbs *much*, *a lot*, *a little*, *a bit* always come after the verb they are describing:

I know a bit about car mechanics.
I'm sure he can help you a lot.

where you have several adverbs in the end position, the usual order is an adverb of manner, an adverb of place and then an adverb of time:

We waited patiently at the bus stop for two hours.
I ran upstairs immediately.

Form

Many adverbs are formed by adding *-ly* to the end of an adjective. For example *quick – quickly* and *helpful – helpfully*.

Some adverbs have the same form as the adjective:

Adjective	Adverb
an early shift	the meeting began early
a fast train	he drove fast
a late start	the meeting started late
a hard worker	he works hard
a straight line	he walked straight up to the front
a direct flight	you can fly direct to Delhi
the wrong spelling	you've spelt it wrong (or wrongly)
a long way	I can't stay very long
the far right	Don't go far!
a near miss	try standing nearer
a daily bus service	the bus comes daily at 9.30
a weekly journal	it comes out weekly

others with the same form are: *high*, *low*, *deep*, *hourly*, *monthly*, *yearly*.

Some adverbs end in *-ly* but have a different meaning from their adjective form:

lately = recently, in the near past
We haven't been to Harry's lately.
hardly = almost none, almost not
I can hardly wait for my birthday!
nearly = almost, not quite
He nearly lost his hat in that strong wind.
directly = immediately, straightaway, as soon as
I'll get in touch directly I have any news.
shortly = soon, in the near future
Tessa is moving to London shortly.
mostly = mainly, usually
He works at home mostly.
highly = very, well, much
They think very highly of your work.

Yet, still and already

We haven't seen the new baby **yet**.

You use *yet* to talk about something which you are expecting to happen but has not happened so far. You use *yet* in negative sentences and in questions and it comes in the end position:

Has he phoned yet? – No, not yet.
We haven't seen the new baby yet.
I can't see Khalid anywhere. – No, he hasn't arrived yet.

You use *still* to talk about something which has been going on for some time and longer than you expected. It comes in mid position in positive sentences and questions but after the subject in negative statements:

I'm still waiting for an answer from my tax office.
Are you still going to Yugoslavia in the summer?
He still won't eat oranges!

You use *already* to talk about something which happened sooner than you expected. You use *already* in positive sentences and questions and it comes in mid or end position:

I've already written and invited them.
He knows about it already.
Have you finished already? It's only 4 o'clock.

Prepositions

He fell off the bridge into the water.

Some very common prepositions that you use are:

at	**special expressions**	at home, at school, at work,
	a particular place	at Piccadilly Circus, at 12 Russell Road, at the cinema, at the back
	a particular time	at 2 o'clock, at midnight, at lunchtime, at Christmas
	after certain verbs	He laughed at me. We arrived at the hotel at 6.
	after some adjectives	She's good at sport.
by	**near/beside**	I left my boots by the door.
	transport	I go by train/bus/car/bike.
	communication	I booked by phone/letter.
	the person or thing that does something	a play by Shakespeare It was struck by lightning.
from	**place of origin**	Where does he come from? from China, from the north, a letter from Jan
	starting point in time	from 9 o'clock until 6
with	**in the company of other people or other things**	I live with my parents. Why don't you go with them? Mix the flour with the water.
	descriptions	a boy with a cheerful face, a car with a black roof
	what you use to do something	Stir it with a spoon. He cut it with the scissors.
	after some adjectives	I'm bored/fed up with school.

Prepositions of time – when?

on	**a day of the week**	on Monday
	a day + morning/ afternoon/evening/ night	on Tuesday afternoon late on Wednesday evening
	a date	on 21 March
	a special day	on his birthday/anniversary on Christmas Day
at	**a time**	at 10 o'clock at midday
	a mealtime	at breakfast at teatime
	a festival period	at Christmas
	special expressions	at night at the weekend at the time
in	**periods of the day**	in the morning/afternoon/ evening/night/day
	a month	in June
	a season of the year	in spring/summer/autumn/ winter, in the summertime
	a year	in 1974
for	**a period of time**	We went abroad for five weeks. I can only stay for an hour. We haven't played for ages.
during	**some point within a period of time**	It snowed during the night. She died during the week.
	certain named periods of time	He fought during the war. during the revolution
on time	**at the right time**	The plane left on time.
in time	**not too late**	The doctor arrived in time to save the injured man.

exact time:

I'll meet you by the clock tower at 10 o'clock.

approximate time:

We'll see you about 10 o'clock then.
(some time just before or just after 10)

general period of time:

The shop is very quiet before 10 in the morning.
The shop gets very busy after 10 o'clock.
The shop is closed for one hour at lunchtime.

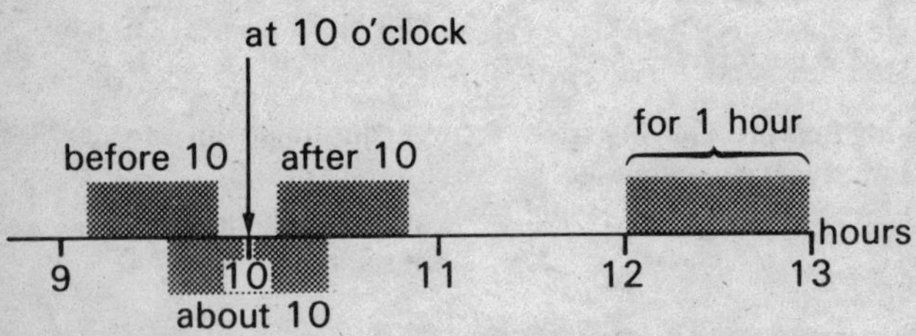

Usage note

Some expressions of time are used with no preposition:

I can't come this week.
Next Thursday will be okay.
We saw them last summer.
I saw him two weeks ago.
We arrived a month ago.

not later than an exact time:

You must be ready by 10 o'clock.
They will have finished all the work by 10 o'clock.
(at 10 o'clock, or some time before)

period of time leading to/from a point in time:

The booking office will be open from 9.30 until/to 5.30.
The shop isn't open until/till 10.
The shop will be open from 10 o'clock.

looking back to the start of a period of time in the past:

I have been waiting since 10 o'clock. (it is now 12)
I've been waiting for 2 hours.
He's been in Britain since December 10. (it is now March)
He's been here for three months.

looking forward to a time in the future, counting from now:

I must leave in two hours (in two hours' time).
She will go to America in three weeks' time.

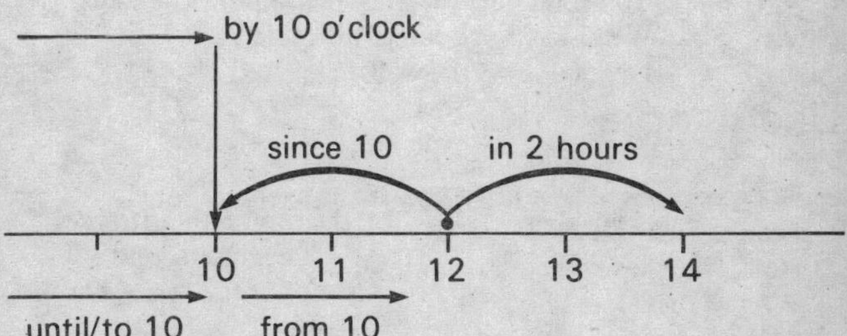

Prepositions of place – where?

behind	Behind our house there's an old wood.
in front of	We park the car in front of the house.
next to	They live next to the butcher's shop.
beside	Sit down there, beside John.
near	The office is near the station – about 200m.
not far from	It's not far from the station – 5 minutes' walk.
outside	I'll meet you outside the theatre.
above	The plane flew above the clouds.
over	They live in a flat over (= directly above) their shop.
below	You can't see the damage. It's below the ground.
under	He hid under the bed.
between	We squeezed in between two tables.
opposite	My office is opposite Mr Jones'.
among	You could just see the house among the trees.
round	We all sat down round the table.
against	I leant against the wall and rested.

at	**an exact position**	at the top/bottom/front/back/beginning/end I waited at the top of the stairs.
	a place	at the cinema/shop/doctor's at the pub/office/bus stop I'll meet you at the station.
	an address	We live at 9 King Street.
on	**a surface**	on the wall/ceiling/floor/shelf
	a line	on the London Road, on the river
	other expressions	on the right/left

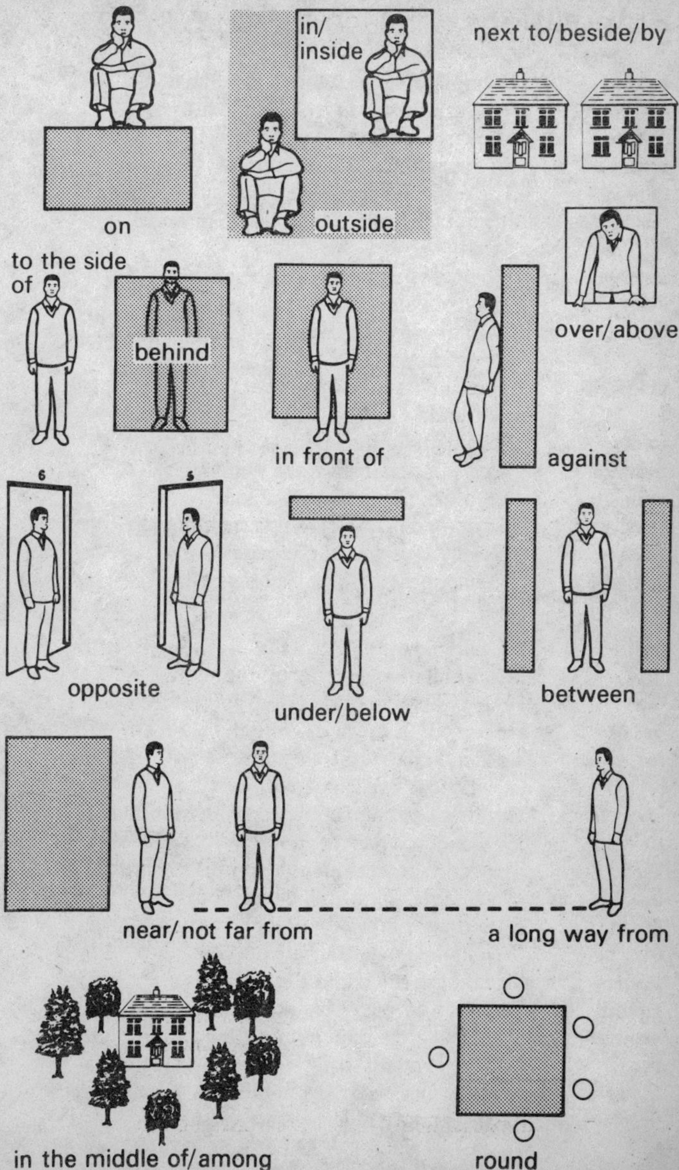
on
in/
inside
outside
next to/beside/by
to the side of
behind
in front of
over/above
against
6
5
opposite
under/below
between
near/not far from
a long way from
in the middle of/among
round

in	**a country, a town, a street, an area**	They live in Spain, in Madrid. She works in Oxford Street. I like shopping in Covent Garden.
	inside a building	There's a cafe in the station. She plays the piano in the pub.
	inside a room a container	He's in the kitchen. in the bin/drawer/fridge/oven in my bag/purse/briefcase He keeps his money in a wallet.
	other expressions	in the middle

Prepositions of place – where to?

Some prepositions of place include movement:

onto	He climbed onto the roof for a better view.
off	Be careful it doesn't fall off the shelf.
into	Henry walked into the room and waved.
out of	He ran out of the house into the fresh air.
towards	As I walked towards the house, I noticed a man trying to open a window.
away from	Hundreds of people rushed away from the fire.
past	He wandered past the house without looking in.
through	The train sped through the tunnel towards Leeds.
up	We climbed up the hill in two hours.
down	Push the car down the slope and try to start it.
over	We climbed over the gate into the field.
under	The mouse ran under the fridge.
round	There's a by-pass which runs round the town.
around	We spent a pleasant hour walking around the park.
near	We drove near the park but we didn't stop.
along	Walk along this road and turn left at the corner.
across	Don't let the children go across that busy road!

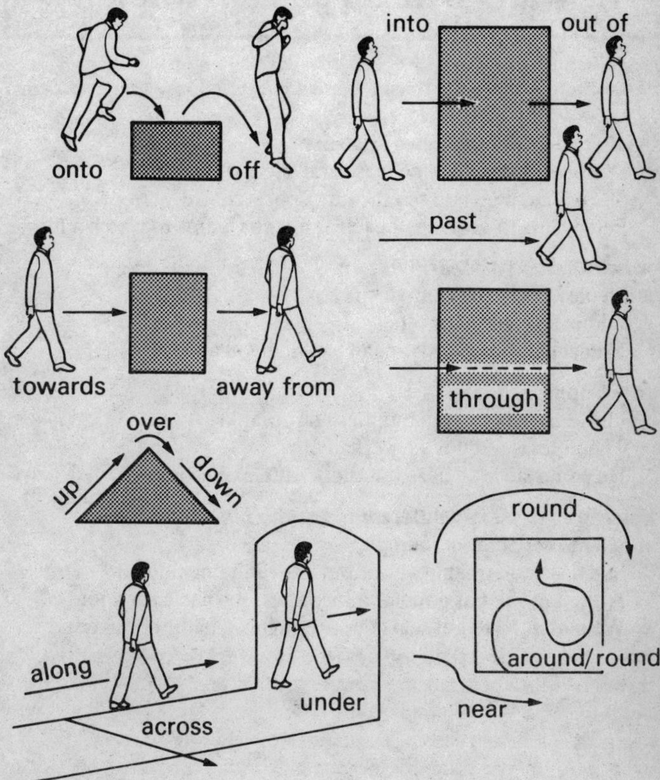
onto
off
into
out of
past
towards
away from
through
over
up
down
round
around/round
along
under
across
near

Conjunctions

He wanted me to go **but** I wouldn't.

***and*, *or* and *but* are the most common conjunctions. You use them:**

to join two ideas or phrases or clauses:

I've bought a piece of cheese and a loaf of bread.
She wants to go and see the new sports centre.
Pete wants to go to the beach and Anna wants to watch a film.

or two alternative ideas:

Shall we take the train or the bus?
I don't like green or blue.
You can use this desk or Jan can find you another one.

or two opposite ideas:

I have milk in my tea but no sugar, thanks.
The hotel is old but very efficient.
He could sleep in here but there isn't much room.

You can contrast two different ideas with *but* or *although/though/even though*:

She has good qualifications but she can't find a job.
Although she has good qualifications, she can't get a job.
We managed to get seats even though we hadn't booked.

Usage notes

When you use *and/but/or* and the subject of both clauses is the same, you often leave out the subject noun or pronoun in the second clause:

The clinic opens at 2.00 and closes at 4.30.
(not: The clinic opens at 2.00 and the clinic/it closes at 4.30.)
I sent them the letter but (I) forgot to enclose a cheque!
Are you selling your car or getting a new one?

You can use other conjunctions to link clauses in different ways:

You can use *so* to explain the result of something:

I didn't like the meat so I left it.
Our homework was too difficult so we didn't do it.
He feels sick so he's decided not to come.

or you can use *so* + adjective/adverb *that*:

The film was so long (that) we had to leave.
He talked so much (that) I fell asleep.

You use *so that* to explain the purpose of something:

You'd better write it down so that I don't forget.
I made some sandwiches so that we wouldn't get hungry.

or you can use an infinitive to show purpose if the subject of both clauses is the same:

He put on an extra sweater to keep warm.
I'm going to the bank to cash this cheque.

You can use *because/as/since* to explain the reason for something:

We didn't go to the seaside because the weather was very bad.
I don't think I'll bother now since it's so late.
As George was the strongest, he led the way.

You can use *if* to introduce the condition for something to be true or possible:

We will come and see you if we have time.
The meat is much tenderer if you cook it slowly.
Can you give him the message if he rings?

and *unless* to mean if . . . not:

You won't get a table on Saturday night unless you've booked.
(. . . if you haven't booked.)
He won't come unless he wants to.

You can use conjunctions to show differences in time:

You can use *as/while/when* to join two actions or activities which happen at the same time:

The fire started in the kitchen while I was watching television.
A dog approached me as I lay on the grass.
I woke up when a car hooted in the street.

You can use *before/after/when* to join two actions or activities which happen at different times:

We had our car serviced before we went to Scotland.
I'll go and see her when/after she comes out of hospital.

You can use *since* to join something back to a point of time in the past:

I haven't seen Gill since I moved to Leeds.
What have you been doing since I last saw you?

You can use *until/till* to join something forward to a point of time in the future:

You must rest until you feel completely better.
Can you look after the shop until I get back?

You can also use the question words *what*, *who*, *when*, *where*, *how*, etc. to join two clauses together. The word order is subject – verb – object after these conjunctions because they are not questions:

I don't understand how he does it so quickly.
We want to find out when the coach leaves.
I'm not sure who the manager is.
Can you tell me where I can buy a paper?

You can use *that* to join the main clause in a sentence to the object clause, but *that* is often left out:

We decided (that) it was too far to drive in one day.
She forgot (that) her parents were coming to see her.
I'm worried (that) it won't work.

Numbers

0	nought/zero/oh		18	eighteen	eighteenth
1	one	first	19	nineteen	nineteenth
2	two	second	20	twenty	twentieth
3	three	third	21	twenty-one	twenty-first
4	four	fourth	22	twenty-two	twenty-second
5	five	fifth	30	thirty	thirtieth
6	six	sixth	40	forty	fortieth
7	seven	seventh	50	fifty	fiftieth
8	eight	eighth	60	sixty	sixtieth
9	nine	ninth	70	seventy	seventieth
10	ten	tenth	80	eighty	eightieth
11	eleven	eleventh	90	ninety	ninetieth
12	twelve	twelfth	100	a hundred	hundredth
13	thirteen	thirteenth		one hundred	one hundredth
14	fourteen	fourteenth	200	two hundred	two hundredth
15	fifteen	fifteenth	1,000	a thousand	thousandth
16	sixteen	sixteenth	1,000,000	a million	millionth
17	seventeen	seventeenth			

You write	**You say**
110	a/one hundred and ten
368	three hundred and sixty-eight
799	seven hundred and ninety-nine
2,554	two thousand five hundred and fifty-four
21st	twenty-first
32nd	thirty-second
103rd	one hundred and third
44th	forty-fourth

Telephone numbers

0223 42556 oh double two three, four two double five six
or oh two two three, four two five five six

How many times?

Take this medicine once/twice/three times/four times a day.
Check the oil level once a month, four times a year, once every three months.

Time

What's the time, please?	It's four o'clock.
What time is it?	It's (a) quarter past four.
Have you got the time, please?	It's exactly half past four.
What time is it now?	It's nearly (a) quarter to five.
What time are you setting off?	About eleven tomorrow morning.
What time did you get there?	It was just gone nine.
When does the Hampton boat leave?	There's one at five past two.
When does the Exeter train leave?	At ten twenty. At twenty past ten.
What time is the bus to Woking?	The next one is at thirteen minutes past six.
What time does the shift finish?	At ten to six.
D'you know when the news is on?	It comes on at two minutes to six.

Usage notes

You only use *o'clock* on the hour:

one o'clock, twelve o'clock

but you can leave it out to be informal: *I'll see you at eight.*

You can leave out *minutes* with 5, 10, 20, 25:

It's ten to three.

It's eleven minutes to three.

You use *in the morning/afternoon/evening* or *a.m.* (before noon) and *p.m.* (after noon) to show which part of the day you mean:

We didn't get back until nearly three a.m.

The race was all over by two thirty yesterday afternoon.

You use *-ish* or *about* to give approximate time:

I should be there by eightish.

I'll drop in about eight tomorrow evening.

Other adverbs you can use with time are *just*, *just gone/after/before*, *exactly*, *nearly*, *almost*.

Days, months, dates

The weekdays	Monday, Tuesday, Wednesday, Thursday, Friday	
The weekend	Saturday, Sunday	
The months	January	July
	February	August
	March	September
	April	October
	May	November
	June	December
The seasons	Spring, Summer, Autumn, Winter	
You write	5.9.84 *or* 5th September 1984 *or* September 5 1984	
You say	the fifth of September nineteen eighty-four *or* September the fifth nineteen eighty-four	

When's your birthday? – It's on the eleventh of August.
When does the new term begin? On Monday the fourth of October.
The Spring Bank Holiday is on the thirteenth of May this year.
The winter sale starts next Saturday at 9 a.m.

Sums and measurements

You write	You say
¼	a quarter of an orange
⅓	a third of the mixture
½	(a) half a packet of pasta, half an avocado
⅛	an eighth of an inch
⅙	a sixth of the annual cost
¾	three quarters of a bottle of wine
.25	point two five
.5	point five
2.75	two point seven five
7½%	seven and a half per cent
10.5%	ten point five per cent
25%	twenty-five per cent
$9 + 17 = 26$	nine plus seventeen equals twenty-six
	nine and seventeen is twenty-six
$63 - 7 = 56$	sixty-three minus seven equals fifty-six
	seven from sixty-three is fifty-six
	sixty-three take away seven makes fifty-six
$4 \times 3 = 12$	four times three is/makes twelve
	four threes are twelve
	four multiplied by three equals twelve
$90 \div 15 = 6$	ninety divided by fifteen equals/makes/is six
25mm	The gap should be twenty-five millimetres wide.
162cm	He is one hundred and sixty-two centimetres tall.
2.5m	The pool is two point five metres deep.
100gm	You need about a hundred grams of ham.
54kg	Kate weighs fifty-four kilos.
10.25l	We are allowed ten point two five litres of wine.
6in	a six-inch gap in the floor
3ft	The table is three feet long.
22yds	My allotment is nearly 22 yards long.
2 miles	It's only two miles to the station.

List of irregular verbs

Base form	Past form	Past participle
arise	arose	arisen
awake	awoke	awoken
be (see page 8)	was/were	been
bear	bore	borne
beat	beat	beaten
become	became	become
begin	began	begun
bend	bent	bent
bet	bet or betted	bet or betted
bite	bit	bitten
bleed	bled	bled
blow	blew	blown
break	broke	broken
breed	bred	bred
bring	brought	brought
broadcast	broadcast	broadcast
build	built	built
burn	burnt or burned	burnt or burned
burst	burst	burst
buy	bought	bought
can	could	
catch	caught	caught
choose	chose	chosen
cling	clung	clung
come	came	come
cost	cost	cost
creep	crept	crept
cut	cut	cut
deal	dealt	dealt
dig	dug	dug

Base form	Past form	Past participle
do (see page 10)	did	done
draw	drew	drawn
dream	dreamt or dreamed	dreamt or dreamed
drink	drank	drunk
drive	drove	driven
eat	ate	eaten
fall	fell	fallen
feed	fed	fed
feel	felt	felt
fight	fought	fought
find	found	found
flee	fled	fled
fly	flew	flown
forbid	forbade	forbidden
forget	forgot	forgotten
forgive	forgave	forgiven
freeze	froze	frozen
get	got	got
give	gave	given
go	went	gone
grind	ground	ground
grow	grew	grown
hang 1	hung	hung
hang 2	hanged	hanged
have (see page 12)	had	had
hear	heard	heard
hide	hid	hidden
hit	hit	hit
hold	held	held
hurt	hurt	hurt
keep	kept	kept
kneel	knelt	knelt
knit	knit or knitted	knit or knitted

Base form	Past form	Past participle
know	knew	known
lay	laid	laid
lead	led	led
lean	leant or leaned	leant or leaned
leap	leapt or leaped	leapt or leaped
learn	learnt or learned	learnt or learned
leave	left	left
lend	lent	lent
let	let	let
lie 1	lay	lain
lie 2	lied	lied
light	lit or lighted	lit or lighted
lose	lost	lost
make	made	made
mean	meant	meant
meet	met	met
mow	mowed	mown
overtake	overtook	overtaken
pay	paid	paid
prove	proved	proved or proven
put	put	put
read	read	read
repay	repaid	repaid
ride	rode	ridden
ring	rang	rung
rise	rose	risen
run	ran	run
say	said	said
see	saw	seen

Base form	Past form	Past participle
seek	sought	sought
sell	sold	sold
send	sent	sent
set	set	set
sew	sewed	sewn
shake	shook	shaken
shed	shed	shed
shine	shone	shone
shoot	shot	shot
show	showed	shown
shrink	shrank	shrunk
shut	shut	shut
sing	sang	sung
sink	sank	sunk
sit	sat	sat
sleep	slept	slept
slide	slid	slid
sling	slung	slung
slit	slit	slit
smell	smelt or smelled	smelt or smelled
sow	sowed	sown or sowed
speak	spoke	spoken
spell	spelt or spelled	spelt or spelled
spend	spent	spent
spill	spilt or spilled	spilt or spilled
spin	spun	spun
spit	spat	spat
split	split	split
spoil	spoilt or spoiled	spoilt or spoiled
spread	spread	spread
spring	sprang	sprung
stand	stood	stood
steal	stole	stolen
stick	stuck	stuck
sting	stung	stung

Base form	Past form	Past participle
stink	stank	stunk
stride	strode	stridden
strike	struck	struck
swear	swore	sworn
sweep	swept	swept
swell	swelled	swollen
swim	swam	swum
swing	swung	swung
take	took	taken
teach	taught	taught
tear	tore	torn
tell	told	told
think	thought	thought
throw	threw	thrown
thrust	thrust	thrust
tread	trod	trodden
undergo	underwent	undergone
understand	understood	understood
undertake	undertook	undertaken
undo	undid	undone
upset	upset	upset
wake	woke	woken
wear	wore	worn
weave	wove	woven
weep	wept	wept
win	won	won
wind	wound	wound
withdraw	withdrew	withdrawn
wring	wrung	wrung
write	wrote	written

Glossary

ADJECTIVE an adjective describes a noun:
This is a *long* road.

ADVERB an adverb describes a verb, an adjective or an adverb:
He speaks *quietly*.
She's a *very* fast walker.

ADVERB PHRASE a group of words which you use like an adverb:
She spoke *in a silly voice*.
They arrived *the next day*.

ARTICLE the definite article *the* or the indefinite article *a/an* is placed before a noun:
a book, *the* road

CLAUSE a clause is part of a sentence with its own verb. The main clause in a sentence is complete on its own:
I'll leave after lunch *when the rain stops*.
The subordinate clause *when the rain stops* adds extra information and cannot appear in the sentence without the main clause.

COLLECTIVE NOUN a noun which refers to a group of people or things:
a *crowd*, an *army*, a *team*, a *set*

COMPARATIVE the form of an adjective or adverb which you use to compare two things:
He is *smaller* than his sister.
He copied *more accurately* than her.

CONJUNCTION a word which joins two clauses, phrases or ideas:
He knocked on the door *but* no one answered.

CONSONANT the letters of the alphabet which are not vowels (the vowels are a, e, i, o, u)

COUNTABLE NOUN a noun which you can count and has a plural form:
houses, *fingers*, *feet*, *trees*

DEFINITE ARTICLE the definite article *the* is used with a noun to identify a particular object, etc.:
the blue car, *the* last house, *the* milkman

DIRECT OBJECT the object of a verb, something affected by the action of the verb:
I saw *him* yesterday.
the object can be a phrase:
He likes *a big dinner*.

ENDING the last letter or letters of a word which change to make e.g. a plural or a past tense:
house*s*, church*es*, kni*ves*, wash*ed*

FORMAL formal English is used in writing and in conversations with people you do not know well and for business meetings and letters when you must be polite and impersonal

FUTURE time after now, which has not come yet

GROUP NOUN a noun which refers to a group of things:
a *class*, a *family*

INDEFINITE ARTICLE the indefinite article *a/an* is used with a noun to name one of a set of objects, etc.:
a blue car, *a* man
we do not know exactly which one is referred to.

INDIRECT OBJECT the object of a verb, but not affected directly by the action of the verb:
I gave *the man* fifty pence.
fifty pence is the direct object, *the man* is the indirect object.

INFINITIVE the form of a verb which often has *to* in front of it, e.g. come:
I asked him *to come* in.

INFORMAL informal English is used in conversations with friends and people you know well, and letters to people, when you do not worry about being very polite and impersonal

-*ING* FORM the form of the verb ending in *-ing*, also called the present participle
He hates *waiting* for buses.

IRREGULAR FORM a verb, noun, adjective or adverb which does not follow the same patterns as most others:
drive, *drove*, *driven* is an irregular verb
child, *children* is an irregular noun

MAIN VERB a verb which can change to show tense or which can form a clause or sentence
I have *lived* here for two years.

MODAL VERB the modal verbs are helping verbs and give extra meaning to the main verb in a sentence. They are *can*, *could*, *may*, *might*, *shall*, *should*, *must*, *will*, *would*

NEGATIVE a sentence with *not*, *n't*, *no*, *nothing*, *no one*, *neither*, etc. is negative:
He does*n't* understand.
other sentences are positive:
I understand your difficulty.

NOUN a noun is the name of something and can be the subject or object of a verb:
The *girl* gave her *work* to the *teacher*.
girl, *work*, *teacher* are all nouns

NOUN PHRASE a group of words which is the name of something and can be the subject or object in a sentence:
the early train, *an old saloon car*, etc.

OBJECT something which is affected by the action of the verb in a sentence:
He raised *his hand*.

PAST time that is finished, the time before now

PAST PARTICIPLE the *-ed* form of a regular verb: *shouted*, *liked*, etc.,
or the irregular form: *saw*

PERFECT a verb form with *have* and a past participle:
He *has seen* the film already.

PHRASAL VERB a verb which has two parts, a main verb and an adverb or preposition:
I'm going to *give up* smoking.

PHRASE a group of words which is not a full clause or sentence:
I've got *a few old things*. (a noun phrase)
He speaks *in a very strange way*. (an adverb phrase)

PLURAL the form you use to talk about more than one of something:
cars is the plural of *car*

POSITIVE a positive statement is definite or certain, without a negative:
He is Italian.
They live in London.

PRESENT the time now, at this moment of speaking

PRESENT PARTICIPLE the *-ing* form of the verb which you use to make the present and past continuous tenses:
He is *reading*.
We were *waiting*.

PRONOUN a word which you use in place of a noun:
he, *it*, *them*, *us*, *yours*

QUESTION TAG a way of asking a question or checking that something is true where you make the question form at the end of a statement:
You understand, *don't you*?

QUESTION WORD words you use to ask questions: *what*, *who*, *where*, *when*, *how*, *why*

REGULAR FORM a regular verb, noun, adjective or adverb forms its endings in the same way as others of its kind:
like, *liked*, *liked* is a regular verb
hill, *hills* is a regular noun

SENTENCE a sentence is a statement, question or command with at least one clause in it: when you write a sentence you begin with a capital letter and end with a full stop (.) or question mark (?) or exclamation mark (!)

SHORT FORM a reduced form of a phrase like *it's* for *it is*, *isn't* for *is not*, etc.

SINGULAR the form you use to talk about only one thing:
car is singular, *cars* is plural

STATEMENT a sentence which gives information, not a command or question:
The train leaves at 10.05.

STRESS saying one word in a phrase or one syllable in a word more loudly than the rest:
It's *Jane* on the phone for you.
ad*ver*tisement

SUBJECT the noun, noun phrase or pronoun linked with the verb:
A man shouted.
He told me to move.

SUPERLATIVE the form of an adjective or adverb which compares something with all others of its kind:
the *oldest*, the *most difficult*

TAG see question tag

TENSE the form of a verb which tells you when something happens, in the present, the past or future time

UNCOUNTABLE NOUN a noun which does not have a plural form because you cannot count it:
milk, *rain*, *bread*

VERB a word which you use to name the action of a sentence:
He *is* ill.
She *works* in the Co-op.
is and *works* are the verbs in these two sentences.

VOWEL the letters of the alphabet *a*, *e*, *i*, *o*, *u*; the other letters are consonants

Index